THE CROOKED TREE

THE
CROOKED TREE

INDIAN LEGENDS AND A
SHORT HISTORY OF THE
LITTLE TRAVERSE BAY REGION

BY
JOHN C. WRIGHT

THUNDER BAY
— P R E S S —

West Branch, Michigan

ISBN: 978-1-882376-34-6

19 20 21 22 23   2 3 4 5 6

Printed in the United States of America
by McNaughton & Gunn, Inc.

DEDICATION.

To those heroic souls, who, plunging into the wilderness at a remote period, paved the way for civilization; yet in many instances did their work without reward, and now lie in obscure graves, this volume is lovingly dedicated.

CONTENTS

CONTENTS

ILLUSTRATIONS

ILLUSTRATIONS

FOREWORD

A tall, crooked pine tree overhanging a high bluff, served to designate what was probably the most important Indian village in the north, prior to the advent of the white man. "Wau-go-naw-ki-sa"—the Crooked Tree could be seen for many miles by the occupants of approaching canoes. After rounding the northwestern extremity of what is now Emmet county, in the state of Michigan, on their way south, it was a familiar sight, and one that never failed to bring exultations of joy from the brave and daring Ottawas. Just where the Crooked Tree stood we have been unable to ascertain; but tradition says it was in the vicinity of Middle Village of the present day. According to the legend it was bent by Na-na-bo-jo. Formerly it was straight, but as the great hunter and chieftain was climbing the hill one day at this point, with his canoe over his head, the end of the boat caught on the tree and gave him a bad fall. In anger he struck the tree a blow with his fist and bent it over. Where he hit the trunk a large swelling came out, and henceforward every knot or growth protruding from a tree was called "Na-na-bo-jo's Fist."

When the French missionaries arrived upon the scene,

they named the place "L'Arbre Croche"; and in the course of time the whole of what is now Emmet county, from Harbor Springs north was known by that appellation. L'Arbre Croche proper was once the center of missionary operations extending over a wide territory, and was the largest Indian village in the region of the Great Lakes. It was situated at a point now called Middle Village, where a mission was established in the latter part of the seventeenth century.

In later years the name L'Arbre Croche was applied to the mission at Harbor Springs.

I am sure that one cannot visit the site of the famous old village without being thrilled with inspirations of nature or overcome by a feeling of sadness at the memories of a departed race. The very trees and stones seem to speak with living tongues of the glory of bygone days, filling the soul with vivid impressions of the place that early association made so dear to the heart of the red man. The delightfully fringed valley and flats below the high hill and along the beach cannot be surpassed for beauty and loveliness of landscape anywhere on the western hemisphere. Shady nooks and leafy bowers, where the Indian lover wooed his sweetheart and told the old, old story over again as songbirds caroled in the branches above, are in evidence on every hand; while long lanes and mossy paths penetrate the forests in all directions. Standing on the shore at the close of day, the magnificent sunset so renowned in this northern country can be seen in all its glory, filling the earth and sky with its splendor and majesty. Verily, the American Indian had a keen appreciation of the beauties of nature.

Annually thousands of pleasure-seekers, tourists and resorters from all parts of the globe roam the paths and forests of L'Arbre Croche, picking up mementoes and enjoying the delightful scenery and balmy atmosphere. The fascinating charm of the whole region gives one an additional zest to learn something of the legends and traditions that have been current among its people from time immemorial. To fill this want, such of the L'Arbre Croche stories as the writer has been able to gather from reliable and indisputable sources are now offered to the public for the first time. Legends, myths, grotesque and ludicrous tales, based upon superstition or imagination, as well as those relating to historical incidents, all had a part in the life of the aborigines of L'Arbre Croche, and are here set down precisely as related by the Indians themselves or by others familiar with their manners and customs.

JOHN C. WRIGHT.

THE CROOKED TREE

ONE THOUSAND MILES IN A
CANOE

In the year 1800 a little girl was born on the banks of Grand river, in the vicinity of what is now the village of Muir. Her father was a noted French trader and her mother an Indian princess, or daughter of a chief. At that period the Grand River valley was one of the most beautiful regions in the whole country, as indeed it is today; and the little girl spent many happy days playing along the shore or paddling in her birch bark canoe. She often accompanied her father on his trips, frequently going with him over portages and rivers as far as Detroit and Chicago.

When this little girl was twelve years of age her father hired two trusty Indians to take her in a canoe from Grand River to Mackinac Island, whither he had preceded her. Drifting down the beautiful river one bright summer's day they emerged into Lake Michigan and turning the prow of their little boat northward started on their long journey. They put up a blanket for a sail when the wind was favorable, and paddled along by easy stages when it was calm. At night they slept by huge campfires, and the little princess heard many tales and legends of savage life.

Origin of the Medicine Lodge

She heard that at one time heaven and earth were connected by a great vine down which fairies and spiritual beings descended to the earth. Mortals were forbidden by the Great Spirit to ascend this vine, but once a young man became sick and in a delirious state climbed up far out of sight. His aged mother was so sad at thus losing her boy that she started after him, but her added weight broke the vine and both came down in a heap. Then the Great Spirit was very angry with the people. "Now," he said, "sickness and disease will prevail amongst you, and instead of living on forever you will die when you grow old. There is only one thing left for you to do. Remember that everything that grows has some value—nothing was made in vain. Therefore you will gather roots and herbs and compound medicines and these will help you when in distress." Thus was born the medicine lodge and all who were initiated into its mysteries were told the above story in great detail wonderfully embellished.

As the canoe proceeded on its way its occupants caught glimpses of roving bands of savages and of deer, elk and wolves as they came down to the lake to drink. Eagles, wild geese and turkeys were seen in great numbers.

When the canoe was caught out on the lake in the darkness the Indians were guided by the stars, and one night the little girl listened with open-eyed wonderment to the pretty legend of the North Star. She had a retentive memory and remembered all these stories. The Indians worshiped her father and did their best to keep their precious charge entertained.

Story of the North Star

Not all Indians believed in marriage, they told her. When a brave refused to wed, others said of him that he belonged to the Two Cousins. This was because, years before, two exemplary young men became very fond of one another and made a vow never to separate. They lived with their grandmother who prepared their meals and dressed their game. But one day the old woman grew weary of her work, and while the young hunters were absent, invited two beautiful maidens from the south to enter the wigwam. When the young hunters returned she said:

"My children, I am growing old and weak. The work of dressing all the game you bring is too great a task; therefore I have asked these two beautiful young women to become your wives, which they have consented to do."

At first the young men knew not what to say. They went about their affairs as usual and made no effort to cultivate the company of the beautiful maidens. But the latter were so pleasant all the time that finally the younger of the hunters fell in love, and the next day when he and his friend started out again to hunt, he could scarcely kill anything because he kept thinking of his sweetheart. He secured only three bear-skins while his cousin took twenty-one.

Then he confessed that he intended to return home and get married.

"If that is the case, I shall leave and never set foot this way again," said the other.

His friend tried to dissuade him, but he started off towards the north.

"Although I leave you," he said, "remember, if you are ever alone at night and need a friend, you will see me up there in the northern heavens. If you ever get lost in the forest or at any time cannot find your way in the darkness, I will always be there to guide your footsteps."

True to his word, be then began to mount up towards the skies, where he assumed the form of a star; and there he is to this day—the bright North Star—chasing the bear as was his wont in the days of old when he hunted through the woods of Michigan.

The other hunter was so chagrined over the loss of his friend that he pined and wasted away before he could reach home, and became only a shadow. Ever since that day he has roamed the hills and valleys and hides from every mortal being among the rocks and cliffs. His name is Bah-swa-way (Echo), and he passes his time by mocking and laughing at everybody.

The two beautiful maidens waited and waited for the return of their lovers and finally in disappointment arose high in the air to watch for them from the skies. They are the Morning and Evening stars.

Day by day the little canoe advanced northward along

the wild shores of Lake Michigan. One day they passed the little stream where Father Marquette had been buried. The old cross was still standing.

Legend of the Sleeping Bear

Not long afterwards they could see the Sleeping Bear Point, and the little princess listened to the story of how in the long ago a great famine had spread over the land. Longingly a mother bear and two famished cubs walked the shore on the Wisconsin side, gazing wistfully at Michigan, which in those days was the land of plenty as it is today. Finally hunger overcame timidity and the bears launched out. Nearer and nearer approached the goal as the mother's words of encouragement urged on the weary cubs.

When only twelve miles from the land of plenty, the mother's heart was rent as she saw a babe sink. With the remaining cub she struggled to gain the beach. Two miles of slow dragging and the second of her cherished ones sank.

The mother reached the beach and crept to a resting place where she lay down facing the restless waters that covered her lost ones. As she gazed, two beautiful islands slowly rose to mark the graves. These were called the Manitous—the home of the departed spirits.

The little princess watched the Sleeping Bear, which was very real in those days, until they passed out of sight.

After awhile they came to a most beautiful indentation of the coast line—Grand Traverse bay. They cut across this to save many miles of travel and camped for the night near Pine River (now Charlevoix). The little girl was not weary nor sad; she was jovial and unafraid. There was real adventure, excitement and lots of fun, too. The Indians told many amusing things. They were not stoical, sullen nor cruel. They saw humor in everything. They told their little passenger of the scheme of the old squaw who wished to appear young.

The Scheme of an Old Squaw

An old woman, wrinkled and decrepit, was seized by the strange hallucination that she still possessed charms sufficient to attract the young men of her village. In this belief she dressed up in her best skins and furs and sat down by her wigwam door, smiling and accosting the young braves as they passed along. Of course none of them paid any attention to her. Then some of the maidens of the tribe, noticing her foolish behavior, went to the old woman and said:

"Look here, Nokomis" (grandmother); "you are old and wrinkled, and your beauty has all faded like that of the dead flowers of the forest. No young man will ever be attracted to your wigwam. You may as well cease all your efforts and live quietly and peacefully, calmly awaiting the end. Your days are numbered; your beauty gone—you nevermore can be like one of us."

At these words the old woman became furious. "Begone!" she said, to her tormentors. "I'll show you whether I am too old or not!"

Then taking a string made from basswood bark, she tied it to the lower part of one of her ears and passing it around the back of her head, drew it taut and looped it over the lobe of the other ear, fastening it securely. In this way she drew all the wrinkles out of her face; and oiling her hair nicely with a mixture of pounded charcoal and grease and drawing it down over the string so the latter could not show, she sat down in the glow of her campfire and waited. The soft light shining on her features which were now smooth and perfect, made her look beautiful indeed.

The first young man to pass that way was immediately fascinated by her appearance, and sat down to visit. The old woman regaled him with many stories and charmed him completely with her wonderful conversation. The next night, and the next following that, found the young man again at the wigwam of the old woman; while several maidens having heard of the strange affair, approached and gazed on wonderingly from a distance. They could not understand the situation at all.

On the third evening, however, while the old woman, beaming with smiles, was talking and making gestures, the string behind her ears suddenly snapped and her face became a mass of wrinkles even worse than before.

The young brave jumped to his feet horror-stricken and bounded out of the wigwam, while the maidens fairly rolled on the ground with laughter. The young man would probably be running yet had he not met a beautiful girl whom he captivated and then led in honor to his wigwam.

The next day our travelers reached Bear River, now Petoskey. There was no settlement on the shore at that time, but there was an Indian village at Bear lake, the source of Bear River (now Walloon Lake). They tarried only a little while, then crossed Little Traverse Bay to the harbor on the north side, called by the Indians Wequetonsing. Here there was only a little high ground and but one wigwam. Farther up the shore, however, was a very large village, the famous Crooked Tree, or L'Arbre Croche of the early French. There our friends were well received and stopped a whole day. Many stories were related and the little princess heard the wonderful tradition of Petoskey and the discovery of the Happy Hunting Grounds.

The next day the voyagers started on what they supposed to be the last lap of their journey. When they arrived at Mackinac the British had invaded the island and a battle was momentarily expected. All was excitement. The little girl along with all the women and children of the island was placed in an old abandoned distillery on the west side for safety. But her father, who thought worlds of his daughter, not knowing what might happen, asked the two Indians if they would not take her on to St. Paul, Minnesota, where her oldest brother was conducting a trading post. At first they refused to undertake so perilous a trip, but his offer was so generous that finally they consented.

Skirting the northern shore of the lake over precisely the route traveled by Pere Marquette, they entered Green Bay, passed through the Fox and Wisconsin Rivers and floated out upon the broad bosom of the Mississippi. They passed through a hostile country where at times they dared not speak above a whisper for fear of being discovered. Their adventures and experiences were many, but at last the faithful Indians and their protégée reached St. Paul in safety. There the little girl remained a few years and then returned to Mackinac over the same route. She was adopted by the famous Madam La Framboise and received a liberal education in French. Afterwards she taught school at St. Ignace for fifteen years. She once entertained President Zachary Taylor; knew Schoolcraft, the historian, and Beaumont, the famous physician; she was personally acquainted with numerous Indian chiefs, sachems and medicine men; she met "King" Strang, Governor Cass and many other notables. She was at home with bishops, scholars and statesmen and was the friend of all.

This little girl with her remarkable experiences and history afterward became the grandmother of the author and related all these stories and many others to him when a lad. The little girl's name was Sophia Bailly, and at Mackinac Island she married Henry G. Graveraet, Jr., the son of a German soldier of the American Revolution and moved to Little Traverse (now Harbor Springs), just previous to the Civil war. From here she often visited the old

Indian village of L'Arbre Croche, where she mingled with the natives and listened attentively to their tales.

Gaw-be-naw, the First Man

The first among the Indians of L'Arbre Croche in story and tradition was Gaw-be-naw. He was said to be the first man created by the Gitchi Manitou (Great Spirit). He ruled over the land and the sea; named all the animals; taught the people how to plant and make gardens; how to hunt and fish; how to build wigwams and canoes; how to count; how to make clothing from the skins of wild animals; and many, many other things. He was a prophet, philosopher, seer and natural born leader.

The snowshoe, bow and arrow, stone tomahawk, pe-no-gawn, "warm winter house," and all such devices and inventions were said to have been introduced by Gaw-be-naw. Volumes could be written of his genius and prowess. No task was too difficult for him to accomplish, no obstacle too great for this wonderful man to overcome. He was greatly beloved by the Great Spirit, who favored him in all things.

Gaw-be-naw lived for a great many years—how long nobody knows. During the early part of his reign all the people were happy; there were no wars, no dissensions— no trouble of any kind. As he grew old and approached the end of his career, however, a great drought and famine spread over the earth. This was sent as a punishment to Gaw-be-naw, who foolishly thinking himself all powerful in his advanced years, tried to make the crops grow without consulting the Great Spirit. In vain Gaw-be-naw fasted and prayed for rain, so that the people would not die of starvation. No rain came, and at last Gaw-be-naw said he would journey to the realm of the Great Spirit and intercede for the people in person.

He traveled many, many days, and at last came to the dwelling place of the Ruler of Creation, who said:

"Gaw-be-naw, my child, you have been very disobedient. I have made you ruler over the land and sea; but I alone have power over the sun and moon, to make the crops grow and the trees to bear fruit. But though you have displeased me I will have compassion on my people. Hereafter Ah-nim-o-kee will sit at my side and when rain is needed he will beat upon his drum. When he pounds with his drumstick, thunder will roll over the earth; when he opens his eyes, lightning will flash; and the people will rejoice, for it will be a sign that I will send water to moisten the ground so that grain will grow in abundance and famine will no longer occur."

So, away past the rivers and mountains, far, far beyond the seas—much farther than man has since traveled, sits an old warrior with his back toward the earth, Ah-nim-o-kee, the Thunderer, who at a signal from the Great Spirit beats upon his drum and flashes his eyes and thus brings the rain to revive and nourish vegetation.

The Lost Tribe of Michigan

The origin of the American Indian has been a subject of speculation and conjecture ever since Columbus discovered the new world. The Shawnees had a tradition that their ancestors crossed the ocean, while other tribes claimed that the race had its beginning in the great northwest. Certain racial characteristics indicate that the Indians descended from the Chinese, some of whom may have crossed into Alaska at a remote period. As related by the historian Shea, one of the early American missionaries, Father Grelon, afterwards went to China. While traveling through the plains of Tartary, he met a Huron woman whom he had known on the shores of the Great Lakes. Having been sold from tribe to tribe, she had reached the interior of Asia. There on the steppes of that distant land she related the wonderful story to her aged pastor. It was this fact that first led to the knowledge of the near approach of America to Asia. Again, the veneration of the wild Indian for the root of the gentian plant was almost identical to that of the Chinese.

Indeed there are some ethnologists who claim that America was the first continent to be inhabited and that Asia and Europe received their original population from this source. They produce geological proofs for such a contention. But these many speculations only lead us on and on into the realm of conjecture. The great outstanding fact is that when the white man came the Indian was here and had many interesting legends and traditions.

The first traces we find of the Ottawas are near the river that bears their name in Canada. Belonging to the Algonquin stock, they early engaged in warfare with the Iroquois Confederation or Five Nations, by whom they were eventually driven westward. Crossing into Michigan at the Sault Ste. Marie River, they came in contact with the Chippewas (or Ojibways), with whom they formed a strong alliance. The two tribes were much alike in manners and customs and freely intermingled. Together they journeyed southward, crossing the Straits of Mackinaw, and by mutual consent the Ottawas occupied what is now Emmet county and founded their village of Wau-go-naw-ki-sa, or "The Crooked Tree."

Farther south they came in contact with the Potawattamies, another similar and friendly people, and the three tribes formed a strong alliance and styled themselves the "Three Brothers." Together they practically controlled what is now the state of Michigan—the Chippewas, the upper peninsula; the Ottawas, the islands and region south of the Straits of Mackinaw as far as Grand river; the Potawattamies, the southern portion. Of course, there were a number of other tribes, such as the Hurons, the Miamis, etc., but as a rule they did not reach far north. Away to the west were the savage Sioux; to the east, the equally bloodthirsty Iroquois; and between the two the "Three Brothers" vacillated with varying degrees of success. At one time the powerful Iroquois cleared the lower peninsula of their enemies as far as the shores of Lake Michigan. At another time, about the year 1671, the Ottawas on the warpath against the Sioux, secured a large supply of arms and ammunition at Montreal; were joined by the Hurons at Mackinac and the Sac and Fox Indians of Green Bay, marched through northern Wisconsin—a well-armed body of over a thousand warriors—and confidently attacked the enemy in the St. Croix valley. Utterly defeated, they retreated through the snow-covered woods, amidst sufferings and privation that equal those of the Belgians of our own day. The heavy loss sustained by the Hurons, who bravely covered the rear, was appalling, and that tribe was greatly reduced. The remnants of the army passed through the L'Arbre Croche country on their way home, and their desperate condition led them to acts of cannibalism.

When the Ottawas first crossed the Straits of Mackinaw on their way south, the territory now comprised in the county of Emmet was occupied by a small tribe of peaceful Indians, known as the Mush-quah-tas, or Underground Indians, so named because they were said to have come from the West, where they formerly lived in caves. They had gardens and comfortable houses and their principal village was located at least five miles from the coast, so as not to be exposed to warlike tribes traveling along the lake. They welcomed the Ottawas and smoked with them the pipe of peace. But trouble soon arose which resulted disastrously for the peaceful Mush-quah-tas and provides the only case recorded in the annals of Indian warfare where an entire tribe of several hundred members, together with the women and children, was totally exterminated in one terrific onslaught.

The Ottawas were in the habit of going on long journeys of conquest, in which they often secured many captives and much plunder from vanquished tribes. These forays were very displeasing to their Mush-quah-ta neighbors, who absolutely refused to aid them in any of their battles. After an unsuccessful raid against the Sacs in Wisconsin, in which they had suffered considerable loss, the Ottawas returned home one summer's evening, loud with wails and lamentations. As they passed the Mush-quah-ta village, some of the young men who were lounging about laughed at them and told them their punishment was well deserved; these young men also foolishly pelted them with balls of wet sand and ashes wrapped up in forest leaves.

This was an insult which no self-respecting Ottawa could endure unchallenged. Sullenly the mourners made their way homeward, stung to the quick by the treatment of their neighbors. Hurriedly summoning a war council, they decided to attack the Mush-quah-tas that night.

An Ottawa maiden, who had fallen in love with a brave of the doomed tribe, discovered the plan and resolved to warn the Mush-quah-tas of their impending fate. Leaving her wigwam at dusk, she undertook to reach the Mush-quah-ta village by a circuitous route, but was detected, overtaken and strangled by two powerful warriors.

As night came on the dark forms of the plumed an painted Ottawas drew close to the wigwams of the sleeping and unsuspecting Mush-quah-tas. Not a sound could be heard except the occasional hooting of an owl or the scurrying of some furry creature through the underbrush Suddenly with a chorus of deafening yells and uplifted tomahawks the Ottawas rushed upon their enemies an began the attack. The Mush-quah-tas, taken at a disadvantage, could offer but feeble resistance. Startled from their peaceful slumber in the dead of night, they bravely reached for their war clubs in a desperate effort to defend themselves. The older men leaped in front of their wives and children and received the fatal blow while protecting their loved ones; the young men made heroic efforts to save mothers, sisters and sweethearts. But it was too late. Bleeding and dying they went down on all sides under the telling blows of the victorious Ottawas. The lost tribe had incurred the enmity of a powerful nation and had to pay the penalty. Only one or two escaped who, with a few families living farther south, journeyed to the present site of St. Joseph, Michigan, where they again established themselves.

Later when firearms were introduced among the Indians, the Ottawas, in a desire to try their effectiveness in battle, hunted up their old enemies, the Mush-quah-tas and exterminated those who had escaped from the former mas-

THE PORTAGE AT L'ARBRE CROCHE

WHISPERS OF LOVE

FRED ETTAWAGESHIK
CHIEF MICHIGAN INDIAN DEFENSE ASSOCIATION

THE SLEEPING BEAR
From the lake the resemblance is striking. It was an ancient landmark when
Charlevoix saw it in 1722.

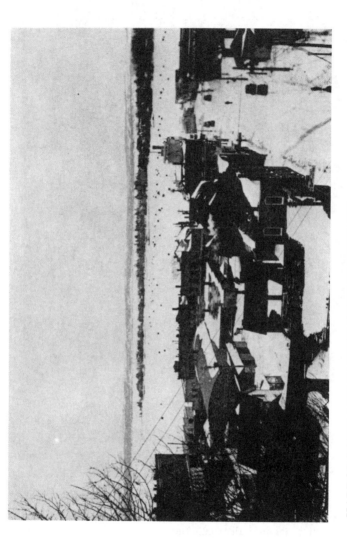

HARBOR POINT AND HARBOR SPRINGS WITH FISHING VILLAGE ON THE ICE

COUNCIL TREE AT TALBOT HEIGHTS NEAR BLISS FARM

Many councils were held around this famous tree in ancient times. One of the largest Indian gatherings in history took place there in 1787. Twenty tribes were represented.

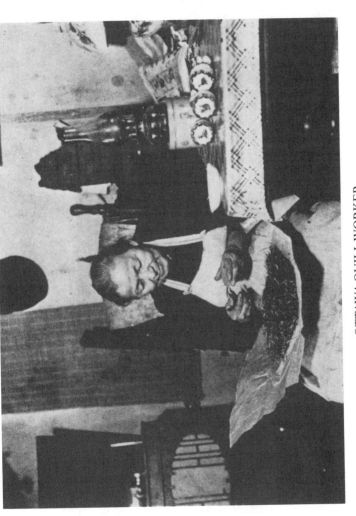

OTTAWA QUILL WORKER

Decorating Indian Bark Work with Porcupine Quills Is Now a Rapidly Vansihing Art

OLD OTTAWA TRAIL AT L'ARBRE CROCHE

sacre. Thus the revenge of the injured Ottawas was deci-
sive and complete and the name Mush-quah-ta become a
synonym for scorn and contempt.

NA-NA-BO-JO, THE OTTAWA WONDER-WORKER

Na-na-bo-jo was a great chieftain with supernatural powers. He performed many marvelous feats and practically all the great natural wonders of the country are ascribed to his ingenuity. To the Indians of L'Arbre Croche and to the Algonquin tribes generally Na-na-bo-jo was a demi-god and miracle man. In some of his pranks he acted the part of clown; many of his episodes were of a humorous nature and generally he was the subject of his own joke. It is hard to understand this character in Indian mythology.[1] While ascribing to him unheard-of and wonderful abilities, the Indians ridiculed Na-na-bo-jo and laughed at his accomplishments. He must not be confused with the Gitchi Manitou, or Great Spirit, of whom the Indians never spoke except with reverence and great respect. Na-na-bo-jo was a wise leader and a sage who benefitted mankind and overcame the power of Evil.

After the Deluge

Many Indian tribes had a tradition regarding a great deluge that once submerged this continent. The Ottawas of L'Arbre Croche say that when Na-na-bo-jo saw that the water had covered all the land and there was no place him

[1] Read "The Geat Myth" by John C. Wright

to set his foot, he caught a muskrat and sent him to the bottom of the sea to bring up some earth. The little animal returned with as much sand as it could carry it between its paws, which it deposited at Na-na-bo-jo's feet. This it continued to do until an island was formed. Na-na-bo-jo made a man out of the ground, which he animated with his breath, and again populated the earth.

Legend of the Great Lakes

As this demi-god was walking along the shores of Lake Michigan one day in search of food, he came to a patch a certain kind of sea weed that he greatly relished. He gorged himself on his favorite dish and lay down to rest. He slept for a long time, until the water, by its gradual movement, had nearly submerged him, and awoke just in time to save himself from a watery grave. He was highly incensed at this action of the water, and, rising to his full height, extended his hands over the lake and said: "Hereafter, that you may fool no one else in this manner, you will become smaller and smaller until you are as draught of water in the palm of my hand."

Since that time the water in the Great Lakes has receded, and it is believed that the day will come when nothing but the great sea basins will remain to show the lakes existed.

Formation of Mackinac Island

Coming to the Straits of Mackinaw, Na-na-bo-jo was at a loss to know how to cross. After pondering some time he decided to build a bridge, which he made from rocks that he picked up along the shore. After he had crossed over, a big wind arose and upset the bridge. The debris sticking up out of the water formed Mackinac Round and Bois Blanc islands.

Joke of the Choke Cherries

Going into the interior of the country, Na-na-bo-jo soon came to a beautiful river on whose unruffled and smooth surface he saw great bunches of delicious red cherries. Bending over to procure them, he plunged into the water head foremost, for what be had mistaken for berries were in reality only their reflection from a tree above. Tearing the tree up by the roots he threw it far to one side, exclaiming:

"Tawa tah! Hereafter your fruit will be black and will parch the throat of whoever eats it." These are the wild choke cherries.

The Chicago-e-sheeg or "Wild Onion"

After a long and painful march through the forest he became very weary and hungry, for he had been unable to kill any game. Coming to a patch of leeks, or wild onion which at that time were very sweet and palatable, he feasted himself liberally, and resumed his journey. He had gone but a little distance, however, when he was gripped with severe pains in the stomach.

"Tawa tah! It's the onions," said he.

Then pulling one up he pinched it disdainfully and said:

"You will now taste and smell strong and no longer be fit for food."

Fooled by His Two Wives

After this he returned home, where he had been in the habit of beating his two wives because they were so dilatory in preparing his meals. But upon this occasion they met him at the door, one on either side, with a bowl of hot min-daw-min-aw-bo,[1] corn soup, in each hand, which they held close to his face and said, "Your meal is all ready, now eat to your heart's content!" Immediately Na-na-bo-jo was all smiles. "Tawa tah!" he exclaimed. "I see you are good wives and I will beat you no more."

Thereafter Na-na-bo-jo and his wives enjoyed great domestic felicity which was promoted in every other wigwam the squaws looking carefully after the epicurean wants of their lord and master.

---

1   "Awbo" is a suffix used in all names of liquids, as peen-awbo for potato soup, jees-awbo for turnip soup, she-min-awbo for cider, ne-beesh-abo for tea, etc.

WHY THE WEATHER IS SO
CHANGEABLE

As those who live around the Great Lakes are aware, this region of the country is noted for its changeable climate. It is common to hear the expression that Michigan has a dozen different weathers in a day. It has always been so, as far back as there are any records to show, and the Indians account for this changeableness of climate by a story they tell regarding Na-na-bo-jo and his brother Pee-puck-e-wis.

These two once ran a foot race from the far south, and from the very start, as was the case in all contests in which he ever had a part, Na-na-bo-jo took the lead. As customary he was happy and pleasant wherever he showed himself, and all nature smiled as he ran along; the sun shone brightly and the birds greeted him with merry songs; little girls threw flowers in his pathway; the squirrels, deer and bears and all animals of the woods came out and gambolled in happiness, saying: "Here comes Na-na-bo-jo, our friend, who makes the pleasant weather."

All summer long he kept advancing northward and every day was warm and bright and there were no signs of frost or any disturbance in the atmosphere. As the contest

proceeded Pee-puck-e-wis, who was angry at being so easily outdistanced, redoubled his efforts and began to catch
up. Then he noticed that everywhere that Na-na-bo-jo went
the weather was beautiful, the flowers bloomed, the birds
sang and nothing interfered with his progress. He became
very jealous and decided to punish the earth and put a stop
to his brother's pleasant journey. So he scooped water up
in his hand and threw it in the air and called on the winds
to aid him in making bad weather. He first asked the south
wind to blow a hot, arid wave that would parch the land
and dry up all vegetation; then he asked the east wind to
bring the rain and cause floods and rivers to overflow; as
he came along he made the clouds gather to obscure the
sun, so that Na-na-bo-jo had difficulty in finding his way.
But at intervals the latter would look back and smile and
the clouds would move aside and allow the sun to shine.
Then Pee-puck-e-wis called on the west wind to bring frost
and hail and sleet. By this time Na-na-bo-jo had reached
the Great Lakes and needed rest. So he camped on the
shore of Lake Michigan, where he arrived some time in
the month of October. Then there was a spell of beautiful
weather again, when the leaves were turning to red and
gold. A sort of hazy, smoky atmosphere settled over the
earth, and for a time Na-na-bo-jo rested and had peace—it
was the period of the glorious Indian summer. But his
brother soon located him, and called on the fierce north
wind to bring the snow and cold, and Na-na-bo-jo had to
hurry on. Occasionally he would look back and smile, and

this would always bring forth the sunshine; but his brother, now close upon his heels, in anger kept calling on the different winds to blow and bluster, and thus it continued until the contestants turned and passed to the far west.

Whenever the climatic changes were particularly frequent and noticeable, the Indians always exclaimed: "Na-na-bo-jo and Pee-puck-e-wis are near by, running their race!"

THE GOLDEN AGE AT L'ARBRE CROCHE

Shortly after the Mush-qua-ta massacre, L'Arbre Croche grew to be a veritable city; together with the neighboring settlements and wigwams lying along the coast, it numbered many hundreds of inhabitants, and became the capital, so to speak, or central point from which all activities in the north were directed. At the time of Pontiac's Conspiracy the great chieftain was informed that L'Arbre Croche would furnish him with nearly 500 warriors—a promise which no doubt would have been kept had not a jealous feeling been aroused by the Chippewas attacking Fort Mackinaw without first consulting the chief of L'Arbre Croche. So populous was the settlement at one time that an Indian might walk a distance of fully twenty miles along the shore and find a wigwam every few rods. Through excavations in the neighborhood, many articles and weapons of copper have been discovered, leading one to the belief that an even older occupancy connected this region with the copper deposits of Lake Superior.

Many ancient cornfields and abandoned apple orchards in the region roundabout L'Arbre Croche attest to the golden age that reigned among these simple people at a later period. Careful investigation convinces us that there was a degree of physical comfort, moral culture and social and domestic happiness among them far exceeding what most people might imagine. Houses of mats, bark and split timber were substantially made and proved not uncomfortable; the "ah-go-beem-wa-gun" was a small summer house for young men, constructed on an elevated platform, and reached by a ladder.

The "o-dup-pe-neeg," native potato, and many varieties of wild fruits and berries grew in great abundance; low marshy places furnished rushes, reeds and tough, fibrous grasses for mats and other household articles; sugar was obtained from the sap of the giant maples in the vicinity, and the bark of the basswood and birch trees was put to innumerable uses. The hunter had to go but a few steps into the forest to secure as much game as he was able to carry home.

The people were morally clean and their rules rigidly enforced. There was no swearing nor bad language used; aged persons were treated with great respect; it was the height of insult for a woman to step over the sleeping or prostrate form of a warrior, and those who did so were severely punished. The gardens were generally at a distance from the village; the owners repaired to them at the proper season, to do their planting and other work, living for the time being in portable tents; the crops were not owned in common, but any persons needing food were always generously supplied by those who were more fortunate.

These people were also the first and original resorters of the Great Lakes region. They spent the warm summer months at or near the village of L'Arbre Croche; the men being occupied by hunting, fishing, in the making of weapons and pipes, or lounging about; the women weaving beautifully ornamented mats in colors, made from rushes and bark of the slippery elm; fashioning baskets, bags, pails, etc., and attending the gardens. But when the cold blasts of winter began to arrive, gradually they migrated toward the south, stopping along the coast as occasion might require, and going as far as the hunting and trapping grounds of northern Indiana and Illinois. Though always attracted by the country immediately surrounding the Great Lakes, they were very active in their movements. Indications of their journeys have been found as far west as the Mississippi river and even at the foothills of the Rocky Mountains. For the most part, each season found them migrating with the birds and enjoying as much prosperity and happiness as the country was capable of producing for a people in their stage of development.

THE INDIAN WHO ASPIRED TO BE PRIEST

The church at L'Arbre Croche prospered under the guiding spirit of its first missionary. After a few months his visits became frequent, and finally he took up his abode permanently among the people he had learned to love. When not occupied by his clerical duties, he visited the Indians in their wigwams and houses, assisting them in various ways, besides instructing them in the arts of peace.

Among other things, be became greatly interested in watching the men and women manufacture different articles from birch bark. From this commodity they made canoes, buckets, wigwams and many utensils for the home. The beauty of its texture and the many layers into which it could be separated suggested to him the idea of making fancy articles to be offered for sale in the marts of commerce. He accordingly told the Indians to color porcupine quills in gorgeous hues, make up many different kinds and sizes of boxes and work out flowers on the bark. Together with a collection of mats, basswood bark bags, etc., he proposed taking these things with him the following spring on a trip to Paris. There he would exhibit the articles and endeavor to establish a regular market for such wares. The Indians went to work with a will and turned out many beautiful specimens of their handiwork.

During these winter days and evenings the missionary became particularly attached to one young man who seemed to excel in whatever he attempted to do. Moreover he had a thirst for the white man's knowledge, which was an admirable trait. The missionary provided him with books and papers and taught him the rudiments of the French language. He learned rapidly, became the priest's assistant in all his work and was a trusted and faithful servant. He had been baptized by the name of "Joseph," but this name not being readily pronounced by the natives, it was corrupted into "Zozep," and he was known to all by that cognomen.

Finally the time arrived for the missionary to depart on his visit to his beloved France. The Indians in their enthusiasm had manufactured many more articles than he could possibly take with him; in fact, there were more than ten persons could have carried in those days of primitive transportation facilities.

He made a careful selection of the best, however, and told them to keep the rest until his return. Before departing he called Zozep to one side and gave him instructions as to what he should do during his absence. He proposed to leave his flock in the young man's care, and appealed to him to do the best be could to minister to his people's wants and keep them in the right path.

Zozep promised faithfully to do what his good father requested. So he was given the keys of the church and the parish house, along with many fervent blessings, and the missionary seemed highly pleased that he could leave his affairs in such good hands. After bidding adieu to each one, and making a final admonition to Zozep to look after everything in a proper manner, he embarked in a canoe with several Indian escorts, to begin his long voyage by the way of Montreal.

About a year elapsed after the missionary's departure, without any word from him, when suddenly the village was thrown into a great state of excitement by the arrival of an Indian runner from Mackinac, who brought word that the priest had returned and would arrive at L'Arbre Croche in a few days. At the appointed time his canoe could be seen approaching the shore, but when he set foot on land, only one or two Indians were on hand to greet him, and the village seemed almost deserted, he asked about the others, he was told that they were all attending church.

"You then have another missionary," he said. "Has one come during my absence?"

"Oh, no," replied the Indians, "they are listening to Zozep."

Forthwith the missionary made his way to the church, and on entering, beheld Zozep attired in clerical vestments, standing in the pulpit and expounding the gospel in his native tongue.

As soon as the missionary could recover from his surprise, he asked an Indian standing near him, how long had been going on.

He was then informed that Zozep had been preaching regularly for several months; had also been hearing confessions and imposing penances.

The priest threw up his hands in holy horror. Summoning Zozep, he reprimanded him severely and demanded an explanation of his strange conduct.

Zozep, smiling blandly, said he thought he was only doing as the priest would like to have him. He had considered it his duty to take full charge of affairs and had told the Indians to be good and threatened them with severe punishment if they disobeyed. Strange as it may seem, the Indians had listened attentively to his sermons and apparently had great confidence in him.

As usual the missionary forgave his protégée, and it has been said, laughed heartily over the affair when the young man was not present. Even after that, Zozep was called on to "make a talk" occasionally, but it is not recorded that he was ever again allowed to hear confessions or don the priest's vestments.

Legend of the Proud Princess

The Indians of L'Arbre Croche had a broad appreciation of humor, especially the kind which placed some despised or hated person in an embarrassing or humiliating predicament. It is said that the braves laughed uproariously as they gathered about the camp fires of an evening and listened to some old squaw relate the following story:

A certain chief had an only daughter, who, by reason of her lofty position, became very proud. She held her head on high and looked with disdain on all the other people of the village, for she thought none of them good enough to associate with her. She said if she ever got married it would have to be with a worthy chief of some other tribe.

Late one afternoon in her self-imposed seclusion she withdrew to the rear of her wigwam, where in a spirit of amusement she made the image of a man out of mud and clay.

"There," said she, after finishing the figure, "you are just as good as all the other men around here. It is indeed strange that such a beautiful creature as I am could make such a homely and ugly looking thing. I can assure you that if you were alive I would never become your wife." And giving it a poke of derision she ran laughingly into the tent.

But the cold air of evening coming on, made the image rigid, and feeling its strength, it suddenly stood erect— a full plumed warrior.

"Tawa tah!" he exclaimed. "How bracing is the cold air. It has made me a great and strong man."

Then thanking the Manitou of the locality for conferring this wonderful favor upon him, he advanced to the wigwam. Opening the flap he cautiously entered and asked to see the chief's daughter.

Her mother, taken by surprise at seeing such a handsome man, hastily summoned the young woman, saying,

"Put on your best garments, my daughter, and be as polite as possible; a handsome man of another tribe has come to see you. Now is your chance—if he asks you to be his wife, do not refuse him."

The girl came forward and fell immediately in love with the noble looking stranger.

He told her he had come from a great distance to claim her and if she accepted him he would be obliged to ask her to return with him at once.

The girl readily agreed to his proposal; as also did the chief, her father. So her mother packed what belongings the bride could carry and the happy couple started on their way.

Everything went well during the cold hours of the night; but when the rays of the morning sun began to strike and warm the hurrying brave he grew faint and sick at heart.

Soon the bride, who was by this time a long distance in the rear, came to a moccasin lying in the middle of the path.

"Why, that belongs to my husband," said she, picking it up. "I wonder how he came to lose it?"

A moment later she came to a legging.

Picking that up also, she traveled on perplexed.

Then in succession she came to his other belongings all strung along the path, first his belt, then his shirt, bow and arrows and war club.

"My goodness, what can have happened to him?" she said to herself.

Soon she stumbled over a foot, then a leg, and at last all huddled up in a little heap was the mud and clay that she had mounded together in the image of a man.

Then she remembered what she had said when she made it, and felt humiliated beyond expression. Turning back, she retreated shamefacedly to her parents' wigwam.

All the young men of the village, having heard of the affair, were lined up to greet her. As she appeared, they laughed and hooted. For days afterwards she felt so ashamed she would not show herself.

Her experience cured her of her folly, and she became convinced that the young men of her tribe were fully as good as those of any other. She married the first one who proposed to her, who happened to be about as homely a man as there was in the neighborhood, but they lived very happily together.

INDIAN MAGIC

There were many feats of magic performed by the Indians of L'Arbre Croche that were truly marvelous. Orders and societies were maintained in which there were different degrees of proficiency, and the secrets were carefully guarded by the magicians and medicine men.

Two feats were commonly practised, in which the magic men were so adept that their fame traveled far and wide, and others considered them little less than supernatural beings. The first was the chees-o-kee, "lodge-shaking," and the other sko-da-Manitou-ka-win, or "going in fire."

In the lodge-shaking feat, the performer, usually an old man, would seat himself in the center of a little wigwam, which was raised from the ground on all sides so that the spectators could see that no one touched it in any way. He would begin chanting and drumming on a tomtom, first slowly, then faster and faster, and finally the tent would commence to sway back and forth, increasing its speed with the music, until it seemed like an animate object; it would shake violently and sometimes the top would nearly touch the ground in its action. The feat was witnessed many times by white people, and a committee of citizens appointed to investigate the matter at Mackinac Island in 1847 reported that it could find no fraud in the exhibition and therefore it must be the result of genuine Indian magic or witchcraft. Some of the more superstitious declared it was the work of the devil.

The feat of "going in fire" was more elaborate, spectacular and awe-inspiring than any other. It had to be performed in the night time and great precautions were taken and wonderful preparations made for it. The magician would assume the form and don the mask of some animal, such as a bear, a wolf or a fox, and anoint his body with certain kinds of oils and extracts. Then starting on a run, he was said to go like the wind and become invisible, except, at intervals, when he would emit a bright light. The practice was usually employed by some evil person who wished to revenge himself upon an enemy. It was said that at a first visit from one "in fire" the victim fell sick and hardly ever failed to die upon the third and last visit, although there were medicines compounded to counteract the effect, which sometimes prevailed if taken in time. It is hard to account for this strange illusion, except on the theory that the liquids with which the body was anointed were of such a nature that they produced a sort of phosphorescent light as the person traveled along. The rest no doubt was the result of imagination and superstition on the part of the on-lookers. Nevertheless, whenever an Indian spoke of "going in fire" it was with abated breath, and anyone claiming to be a victim of this strange custom would grow pale and ghastly at the thought, enduring all manner of mental torture and anguish.

The missionaries always deplored these practices among the Indians and did all they could to discourage them, but in spite of their efforts the customs continued for many years, and were common at L'Arbre Croche as late as 1860 and 1865.

SELECTING NAMES FOR THE INDIANS

Upon one occasion a large crowd assembled at the village to witness some of the feats of the medicine men. The performance continued for several days with great interest, so much so, in fact, that the priest in charge of the mission decided that something would have to be done to counteract the effect. So he proposed to some of the older Indians that if they would abandon their work of magic, which was displeasing to God, he would call a big meeting and give each one a name, the same as the French and English people had, by which they would be known for all time after.

The Indians assented and adjourned from their own meeting place to a location near the little church.

After an effective and proper ceremony, the Indians who wished white names seated themselves in a row upon the ground, Indian fashion, and the priest proceeded by asking the first one what name he preferred.

"Maudit chien," said the Indian, in all earnestness, repeating the French words for "damn dog."

"Oh, that is terrible!" exclaimed the good father; "you must never say such bad words."

"What name do you wish?" he then asked, turning to the next.

"Sacre crapo" (cursed toad), was the reply.

"Mercy," said the priest, "I'm surprised at such vulgarity. I cannot give you a name like that." And with a look of disgust he passed on to the next.

"I hope you have selected a better name than the others," he said.

"Pauvre diable" (poor devil), was the reply.

"What infamy," said the priest, wringing his bands and passing on.

The next Indian wished to be called "enfant de l'enfer" (child of hell), still another asked the sobriquet of "tête d'escabo" (blockhead), and so on, clear around the circle.

At length the missionary raised his hands on high in despair. "What can be the trouble with all these poor people?" he exclaimed. "Where did you learn such bad language? I never heard its equal before!"

"Those are the words the Frenchmen use," replied the Indians, "and we supposed they were fine words, they use them so much. We've learned them all by heart, and we thought they must be grand names."

"You are very wrong," said the father, "those are not good names but bad ones." He then explained to them the words and their meaning, and afterwards selected suitable and appropriate titles for all, with which they were baptized. The latter names are those that are still common among the natives of this region.

For many years the custom also prevailed at L'Arbre Croche of giving Indian names to white people. Those who wished to be so honored would state their desire to the chief and the names would be conferred upon them at an appointed feast with suitable ceremonies. The names selected by the Indians upon such occasions were generally very appropriate, often indicating the man's business or some peculiar trait of his character; sometimes they were not highly complimentary, but were always accurate in designating the person to whom applied.

A leading merchant of the village once expressed his desire to have an Indian name and was accordingly invited to a feast given for the purpose. This merchant was not particularly popular among the Indians, who considered him very penurious and inclined to be tricky in his dealings. Nevertheless the ceremony proceeded with much jollity and at last he was told that he was to be named "Bub-big."

He was very proud of the name and repeated it over many times. He lost no time in telling his friends about it and all congratulated him upon the honor, because, it must be stated, only leading citizens, as a rule, could aspire to be thus christened at a public feast.

But finally the thought struck him that he would like to know what the name meant in the Indian language. He accordingly asked a native who entered his store soon after, what the word "Bub-big" meant. He was at once told that "Bub-big" meant "flea," and though he was not as proud of his Indian name as before, it clung to him ever after.

THE TOAD WOMAN

Me-non-a-qua[1] came out of her wigwam, took the highly embroidered tick-i-naw-gun (cradle), in which her pretty baby was tightly laced, and hanging it on the limb of a nearby tree, started toward the spring a few rods distant for a pail of water.

At that moment the face of old Muck-kuk-kee-qua (toad woman) peered through the bushes, and as Me-non-a-qua disappeared from view down the pathway, she quickly darted out, seized the tickinawgun with its precious contents and ran towards her hut across the valley.

When Menonaqua returned and discovered that her baby was gone she was overcome with grief and set up a loud lamentation. She had carefully guarded the little one since its birth and had been enjoined by her husband, the great chief, that very morning, before he departed on his hunting trip, not to leave his son alone a moment lest he be kidnapped by some evil person. The child was so perfect and pretty it was the idol of its father.

---

[1]   The suffix "qua" indicates the feminine gender in the Ottawa language. Though she might have another name, a man's wife could always be designated by adding "qua" to his name. It is also the root word of "squaw," but is properly pronounced with the "a" long.

Menonaqua lay moaning at the entrance of the wigwam when the chief returned home. She had not the temerity to tell him what had occurred; but not seeing the tickinawgun, he mistrusted that something terrible had taken place, and half surmising the truth, demanded:

"Where is my son?"

"Oh, my husband, don't be angry. I left him hanging on a tree while I went after water, and though I was gone but a moment, when I returned the baby and tickinawgun had disappeared."

"Miserable woman!" said the chief, "you are not worthy to be called wife. I will go in search of my boy and if I fail to find him by nightfall, I will leave you, never more to return."

In vain did the old man follow every trail, he could find no trace of the missing child; and thenceforth Menonaqua was left to shift for herself. She was lucky to get off with her life, her husband was so incensed.

Many years passed and through brooding over her misfortune, Menonaqua grew thin and wrinkled. Food becoming scarce in her neighborhood, she finally decided to cross the valley and make her home near that of old Muck-kuk-kee-qua.

One day her son, who had grown to be a man, told the toad woman, whom he thought was his mother, that he had seen a strange squaw near by, and she looked so pitiful that he wanted to go and give her something to eat.

"Oh, don't have anything to do with that old Zee-go-wish" (wrinkled face), said Muck-kuk-kee-qua.

"Why do you hate her, mother?"

"I don't hate her, but she's a busybody."

"Please give her to eat for my sake?"

After a number of entreaties the toad woman took the brisket of a deer and going towards the newcomer's hut called from afar: "Zee-go-wish! Zee-go-wish!"

The other answered faintly, "What is it?"

"Seeing we endure your presence, take this and be thankful for it. Now I hope you'll be satisfied!" exclaimed Muck-kuk-kee-qua, turning on her heel.

"Me-quach" (thank you), said the other meekly.

While returning from a successful hunt loaded with deer meat a few days later, the young hunter passed close to the hut of the strange woman, and looking in at the door, saw a face at once so pathetic, sweet and affectionate that irresistibly he felt himself drawn toward it. Looking up, Menonaqua recognized her long lost son and exclaimed: "Oh, my dear boy, come in and do not shun me, for I am your mother."

"How can that be?" asked the young man, "Muck-kuk-kee-qua claims that I belong to her."

Then Menonaqua told him the story of his being stolen when a child and how his father, the great chief, was so angry that he left her forever on account of it.

"That you may know that I am telling the truth," she

said, "ask the Toad Woman to show you the tickinawgun in which she carried you when a babe. Then ask her to show you the tickinawguns of her other children. You will see how much more beautiful and nicer yours is, which will prove to you that you are the son of a chief and not descended from a Toad Woman."

"I believe you, mother," said the boy. "Take this venison and I will go and question old Muck-kuk-kee-qua."

When he arrived home he said to the Toad Woman, "See here, mother, I have never seen the tickinawgun in which you carried me when I was little. Won't you please show it to me?"

"Why are you getting so inquisitive all at once?" she asked in wonderment.

"Oh, I just happened to think that I would like to look at it."

"I'll bet you've been to see that old Zee-go-wish. I'll show you the cradle, but don't go near that 'old wrinkled face,' again on peril of your life." Then she hobbled away and presently from among a pile of furs and skins she produced the prettiest tickinawgun he had ever seen, embroidered with quills and decorated with beautiful ornaments.

"There," she said, "is what I carried you in when you were a child."

After admiring it he said, "Now will you please let me see the ones you carried my brothers in?"

"This is surely the work of that mischievous old hag," said the Toad Woman, but being afraid to arouse the suspicions of the young man, she again hobbled away to get the other cradles. Soon she appeared with two dirty and common looking affairs which the said were the tickinawguns in which his brothers had been carried.

"How is it?" he asked, "that mine is so pretty and theirs so dirty and homely?"

"My, but you are impudent to be asking so many questions. But you were better looking, that's the reason."

"Yes, and that's what always has puzzled me, mother. Why are my little brothers all so black, small and ugly, while I am so different?"

"I guess 'old wrinkled face' has put it into your head to ask me all these questions, thinking to embarrass me; but I am used to such tricks. I will answer your questions truthfully and prove that I am not trying to deceive you. When your brothers were born, the weather was cold, dark and dreary; and that's why they are small and inferior looking. But when you were born, the sun was shining brightly; the day was warm and cheerful. For them I used the old tickinawguns, but for you I had to have something better."

"Very well, mother," said the young man, "now I am satisfied. I killed a big deer at the end of the path yonder, but was so tired that I could not bring it home with me. I wish that you would go and get it."

"I'll do so," said Muck-kuk-kee-qua, "but don't you dare play any tricks on me. If you do, I'll make you and

Zee-go-wish pay dearly for your fun."

After she was far out of his sight, he caught all his little brothers, of whom there were eighteen or twenty, and stringing them on a pole, hung them high up in the crotch of a tree in front of the wigwam. Then going and getting his real mother he set out with her in search of his father.

When Muck-kuk-kee-qua returned towards evening all tired out from her fruitless quest of the deer and saw what had been done, she was wild with rage. She unstrung her children, but their backs were so bent and their hips so twisted that all they could do was to hop around and turn somersaults. She tried to take them with her in pursuit of Menonaqua and her son, but could make no progress— she, too, had been turned into a toad and could only hop and jump around in the dirt, like her children.

The young hunter who escaped with his mother soon succeeded in locating his father, the great chief. He reconciled his parents, who again lived together, but no more tickinawguns were left hanging on the trees.

WHY THE PINE TREES WEEP

Fifteen or twenty years ago there lived at Manistique, Michigan, a full blooded Indian, by the name of "Cornstalk," who was considerably past one hundred years of age. He was on Mackinac Island during the War of 1812 and could tell many thrilling and interesting stories. He was a unique character on the streets of the northern Michigan city, and possessed wonderful vitality for one of his advanced age.

In his younger days Cornstalk had an experience which tried his nerves. One bitter cold day in the winter time a tree fell on his leg, pinning him to the ground. No help was near. He couldn't move, and he knew if he remained in that position long he would freeze to death; so he reached in his pocket for his knife and cut off his leg, and then crept home on his hands and knees.

Cornstalk related the following quaint but pretty legend, explaining why drops of water, like rain, sometimes fall from pine trees:

Mongo, according to Cornstalk, was the first man that inhabited the earth. He came from the land of the rising sun and made his home along the streams of the north and the shores of the Great Lakes. Although fish and game were plentiful, Mongo was dissatisfied and lonesome, for he had no companion to share his joys. The Great Spirit saw that his heart was sad, and one night as Mongo sat in front of his wigwam warming himself by a huge camp fire, he was suddenly startled by a bright light in the heavens; and on looking up saw a meteor swiftly descend to the earth, leaving a train of flames in its wake. The bright ball fell only a short distance from where he was seated and as it fell it burst into many pieces and a beautiful woman stood before him.

Mongo was frightened and would have fled, but the woman held out her hand and beckoned him to come. Mongo's fear suddenly left him and a new, strange passion—that of love—took its place and filled his soul. He led Wasaqua—which name means the new born light—to his wigwam on the banks of the "roaring Escanaba," where for many moons they lived together happily and several children were born to them to bless their union. But one day Mongo became sick and although Wasaqua nursed him with all a woman's tender care, he sank rapidly and ere many days he died.

Wasaqua was inconsolable. She lay upon Mongo's grave and wept and dampened the earth with her tears. She refused food and would not be comforted. The birds and beasts brought her many tender morsels, but she put them aside.

At night bears and wolves lay down by her side to keep her warm; but her grief kept increasing until nature could stand it no longer and she fell into the sleep that knows no waking. She was laid in the grave by the side of her husband at the end of the day; and the whippoorwill's voice was hushed and the howl of the wolf echoed not through the forest, so great was the grief of all living creatures.

But before the sun shone upon that grave again, a great pine, like a solitary, watchful sentinel, stood at the head of the mound where the first man and woman were returned to earth "to mix forever with the elements."

The pine was the first of its kind among the monarchs of the forest and night and day it wept and sang a sweet, sad requiem o'er the lonely mound. And to this day the pine trees weep and moan and sigh for the first born of the earth.

It is a singular fact that pine trees easily gather moisture which slides off the "needles" in the form of rain; but the Indians think it is Wasaqua's tears which she shed on the grave of Mongo.

RAPID TRANSIT IN EARLIER DAYS

"De Hinjum do funny trick," said Napoleon Tebo, as we were paddling down a river one morning in late autumn.

"Old Pere Tebo," as he was called—the last of the coureur de bois of the north country—was a man of unusual hardihood, and his knowledge of hunting and trapping and the early life of the woods was inexhaustible.

The above remark was in response to a request I had made to tell me one of his many thrilling experiences, and as he took his short clay pipe and proceeded to puff long wreaths of smoke, I settled back comfortably to let the canoe drift lazily with the current; for I knew I was about to hear some choice bit from the Frenchman's repertoire.

Fond as I was of fishing, I would rather sit and listen to Pere Tebo tell a story in his inimitable patois than to haul in the gamiest black bass in the river.

With his dark, wrinkled, oval face drawn into innumerable contortions as he sat and related his tales he seemed to me to be a worthy rival of Robinson Crusoe or King Arthur's Knights of the Round Table.

"Dey can put medicine on dare skin," he continued, "shoot fire out dare eyes an' run t'ru de woods like wil' animal. Dey scare de dev out anyone dey meet."

"Did you ever see one do such a thing?" I questioned, by way of further drawing him out.

"I see him do it good many times, me. When I was carry de mail on Shushwar an' Mackinac I take trip of hover hundred miles on lil' piece bark in jus' t'ree, four hour. By Gee Pwell, we go like lightning. Din't I never tole you dat, Misseu?"

"No, Pere, I never heard a thing about it."

"Well, I'm sprise. I t'ot heverybody knowed dat. You see, I have to take long trip wid dog and tranneau. I go on Cheboygan, pas' Hinjun River, clear on de Gran' Traverse Bay. De snow was ver' deep an' de road ver' bad. But eet makes no difference, de mail she has to go so long as ol' Pere Tebo ees able to carry heem.

"We'en I come on Gran' Traverse Bay I was 'bout five hour late an' all tire out. I wish for rest, but my wife was seek w'en I leave him on Petite Traverse an' I'm een great hurry for get back. After I change de mail bag de ol' chief of de village come an' ask me for go on his wigwam an' have bowl hot corn soup. He say, 'You need dis to brace you up before you go back.' My, eet was taste bon— de Hinjun know how to make de corn soup. But eet take Frenchwoman to make de pea soup, ees dat not right, Misseu?"

I nodded assent, as Pere Tebo relit his pipe, took two or three puffs and continued:

"Den de chief say I better lay down for lil' res'. Eet ees long trip an' I'm liable for exhaus'. De dog also ees een no shape to travel so far. I feel so tired I say, 'I'll lay down li' while but not long—I'm anxious for get home.'

"I was hardly stretch out on de fur, we'en all at once dare was big light. I see my house on Petite Traverse an' my wife on hees bed so seek he can't stan' up. 'Nap,' he says; 'Oh, Nap, come an' help me—I'm goin' die.'

"I jumped on my feet an' tell de chief I'm goin' hetch up my dog an' start for home.'

" 'No,' he says, 'wait teel morning.'

"I tole him my wife was seek an' I have to come right off. Maybe I get dere too late an' he be dead. Sacre!'

"'Too bad,' the chief say. 'I help you go quick.'

"Den he take some dat maudit grease an' he rub it all hover my body. Den he put some on lil' piece of birch bark an' tole me to sit down on de bark.

"Den he pass his Han' hover my head an' say something in Hinjun. I no understan' but all at once I feel myself sailing 'long de groun' fas'er dan lightning. We pass by house an' wigwam so swif' eet look like long street. I try for holler or make noise to attrack some of my frien's as we go by, but my face act like she have lockjaw. I can't hopen my mout' even for say bon jour. Sacre, but we was fly!

"I see spark fly 'round an' look under me an' de bark seem all on fire but she no burn. W'en I look 'roun' I see long track of flame follow behin'.

"I was feel awful scare an' begin to wish I was back on Gran' Traverse bay; we'en all at once I see nudder big light which show my house on Petite Traverse. I see my wife seek on de bed wid his Han' stretch out toward me an' holler: 'Oh, Nap, I wish you be here now. Hurry, back, fas' you can, I'm so seek I got to have de physich. Can't you hear me, Nap? Don't stay on de Hinjun house long de road, but come to me quick as de tranneau will carry you!'

"Dat give me couragement an' I say, 'All right, Angelique, wait lil' while an' Napoleon will be on deck.'

"De bark seem to understan', too, an' give jump an' go fas'er dan ever.

"My heart come up into my mout' an' I say to myself: 'If I can only get home before my wife die, I'll be happy man; 'so I hang on wid all my might an' say to de bark; 'Go fas' you like—I'll be scare no more.'

"Before we go far I see lights an' I know I'm near home. De piece of bark sail 'long de track jus' like she be alive—pas' lake, hill an' river an' never make mistake nor take wrong path. Before I know it she sail right up to de door on Petite Traverse an' stop.

"I jump out an' run on de house an' go to the bedroom an' my wife set up an' say, 'Oh, Napoleon, I'm so glad you come. I have bad dream. How you get here so quick? I t'ot you mus' be far 'way on Gran' Traverse. I'm awful seek an' I t'ot I die before I ever see you again.'

"I look at de clock an' eet was only two een de morning. I lef' Gran' Traverse after 'leven o'clock dat evening so I make de trip een about t'ree hours—over sixty mile.

"I tole Angelique 'bout de chief an' de lil' piece of bark, an' she say, 'No one can do dat, Napoleon. You mus' be mistake.'

"I say, 'No, ma chere, dare ees no mistake, I go out an' bring you de bark.'

" 'All right, Nap,' he say, 'bring de bark, I like to know how he Hinjun do dat trick.'

"So I go out for get de piece of bark, but sacre! she disappear. Nobody will believe me now. I feel awful sorray.

"I go back an' tell my wife, 'De bark ees gone.'

"'I guess you must been drunk,' she say. 'If eet was true story de bark would be dare.'

"'Now I remember it,' I say. 'De Hinjun chief w'en he rub on de medicine he talk to de bark. I din't know what he say den. Now I know. He tole it to make return trip—dat's why she's disappear."

AN INDIAN LAWSUIT

A very unusual thing once occurred at L'Arbre Croche. An Indian by the name of Duny-age-ee, in a fit of jealous rage, killed his cousin, a beautiful maiden of sixteen summers, near the outskirts of the village. In the dusk of evening he had followed her down a secluded pathway, whither she had gone in search of some pitchwood, with which to start a fire. When she discovered that she was being followed, she started to run, but Duny-age-ee was close upon her, and by his superiority as a runner soon reached her side. They were just entering a little gully, where all was dark and quiet, when the man seized the maiden by the arm and demanded that she go with him and not resist, or he would kill her. But the young girl was brave and supple, and not to be easily intimidated nor coerced. Proudly raising her head, she drew her hunting knife and defiantly faced her enemy. With a sneer, he wrenched it from her hand and threw her to the ground. Her struggle was long and heroic, but at last the superior strength of the man asserted itself and when the stars and moon peered through the trees they beheld her lifeless body lying prone and bleeding in the bottom of the gully. A dark form scurried down the pathway, looking neither to the left nor to the right, and an owl hooted dismally from a nearby tree. The deed was committed in the darkness of the night and the criminal escaped in the recesses of the forest.

The Indians were sufficiently civilized at this time to fully realize the enormity of the act, and the following day the entire village was aroused to a high pitch of excitement. A search was instituted, the fleetest men of the tribe were sent out in all directions, and finally Duny-age-ee was captured. The friends of the murdered girl were then consulted and expressed a desire that he be punished as the white people punish their criminals. Not having any methods in their native customs of disposing of such cases, except by barbaric forms, the head men went for advice to Colonel Boyd, a white-haired veteran of the war of the American Revolution, who resided at Mackinac Island, and who had much influence among them. After carefully considering the matter, Mr. Boyd advised them to mete out to the prisoner whatever punishment they found he deserved by some proceeding of their own. Whatever they would do, he said would be all right.

After much consultation, the chiefs decided to hold a lawsuit. So a large wigwam for the occasion was built on the hill at L'Arbre Croche, where all the relatives of the murderer and his victim, their friends and a number of onlookers, assembled one fine summer's day, in an endeavor to satisfy the ends of justice and firmly establish the social order, from the aboriginal point of view.

On either side of the tent were long benches, the brothers and sisters and near relatives of Duny-age-ee sitting on one side, and those of the murdered girl facing them on the other; the oldest member of the respective families being seated at the head, and so on down to the foot according to their age.

At the head of the wigwam, on an elevated platform, sat A-pock-o-ze-gun, the great chief of the Ottawas, his person ornamented with eagle feathers, silver medals and beads and wearing his beautifully embroidered blanket, as was customary at great events. In the center of the room were great piles of furs, blankets, tobacco, guns, ammunition, etc.; outside were horses, cattle, in fact, everything that the Indians considered wealth, brought there by the relatives of Duny-age-ee to buy their kinsman's liberty.

When the time for the trial arrived, Chief A-pock-o-ze-gun arose and made a short, eloquent speech in his native tongue. He said that they were not gathered to avenge the murdered girl, as their priest taught them that God, the Great Spirit, would do that; but they were there for the purpose of making peace between the estranged kinsmen. He then produced a calumet, "long pipe," which had been handed him by one of the medicine men present, and, filling it with tobacco, lit it by the means of flint and steel. After he had taken a long puff he presented it to the first of Duny-age-ee's relatives (his father), who took it and smoked as a token of peace.

The chief exclaimed, "Me-sa-gwa-yuck," which means "that's right," and passed it on to the next, who likewise took a puff, and so on, to the end of the row; no one refusing the pipe of peace.

The chief then said, "These relatives of the prisoner, you see, desire peace and not bloodshed. They are sorry for what has been done, and have brought all these goods, which they offer to the family of the dead girl, so that they will have compassion and not ask for revenge."

He then passed the pipe to the first one on the other side, the oldest sister of Duny-age-ee's victim. After some hesitation, she took the proffered pipe and smoked. Three other sisters followed her example, also her three oldest brothers, and the pipe was handed to the eighth and last relative, the departed girl's favorite brother, a young man who sat with flashing eyes at the end of the row.

Shaking his head he said, "Kaw" (no), and refused to smoke.

The chief looked downcast and muttered, "Sun ah gut" (too bad), and taking the pipe, carefully emptied it of all its contents. Then filling and lighting it as before, he again handed it to the young man.

"Kaw! kaw!" repeated the latter, indignantly.

"Gitchi sun ah gut!" (much too bad), exclaimed the chief.

The young man jumped to his feet and pointing to the prisoner, threatened him with his life. Turning to his brothers and sisters, he rebuked them fiercely, saying that for the few paltry articles that were offered them they were willing to sacrifice their relative, but as for him, he would not rest until he had killed the villain and avenged his sister.

The friends of Duny-age-ee advised him to flee at once, lest the brother kill him, and some of them helped him to escape. He was taken through the forest to the lake, placed in a canoe and told to paddle far, far from L'Arbre Croche. He remained away for many years and did not return until the man who had sworn the vendetta was dead.

In some respects the lawsuit showed wisdom and considerable judicial ability, but was indecisive, because the unforeseen had happened—the jury failed to agree.

HOW THE INDIANS SELECTED A
PICTURE FOR THE ALTAR

When the second church was erected at L'Arbre Croche, the missionary who had the matter in hand requested the Indians to provide suitable decorations for the altar. They promised to furnish what was necessary, and the good priest, who had other missions to visit, departed joyously on the rounds of his journey. As winter was approaching, the Indians were soon on their way to the south. There they met a French trader who had in his possession, among other articles for sale, a beautiful oil painting, depicting a courtier of the reign of Queen Anne presenting a rose to his lady love, in true knightly fashion. The picture at once took the fancy of a young Indian, who suggested to his people that they procure it to hang in their beloved church. His advice proved acceptable to the others, and the following spring found the painting hanging over the center of the altar, which was profusely decorated with paper flowers of all colors and varieties and many other gewgaws and trinkets.

In due course of time the missionary visited his other churches and returned to L'Arbre Croche. He was royally welcomed by the people, who informed him that everything was prepared to begin services whenever he should be ready. But upon entering the little church he was horrified to see what had been done; for the lady in the picture, according to the artist's fancy, was attired in the extreme fashion of her day, with low cut dress and short sleeves. Imagine, if you can, such a picture in a house of worship! The reverend father stood for some time, alternately overcome by astonishment, vexation and chagrin, then calling some of the leading Indians to one side, told them he was very sorry, but the picture they had procured was not suitable for a church; that it was a most beautiful painting and a credit to their foresight and generosity, but a secular representation of such a character could not be allowed in the house of God.

Greatly disappointed, the Indians withdrew, called all the people together, told them what had been said, and a long and earnest consultation was held.

Finally a spokesman was chosen, who was sent to the priest to tell him that in spite of his objections the picture was very pleasing to them; they were unable to see any harm in it or anything wrong, and should it be removed, after all the trouble and pains they had taken to secure it, they would consider it an unfriendly act; and many members of his congregation, it was feared, would be so displeased that they might remain away from the church altogether.

The Indians waited in a body, a short distance away, for his reply.

Then the forgiving and kind father, realizing the true situation and the innocent intentions of his as yet uncivilized children, sent word that the picture would not be taken down, and for them to all come in and attend Mass. They gladly accepted the invitation, and the picture, which was a Murillo, remained where the Indians had placed it for many years.

LEGEND OF THE MOTCHI MANITOU

The Indians of L'Arbre Croche were firm believers in manitous, or spirits. All the good things they attributed to the Gitchi Manitou (Great Spirit); and the bad things to the Motchi Manitous (Bad Spirits), there being very many of the latter.

The Motchi Manitou, most dreaded in these parts, inhabited the waters of Little Traverse Bay, and many frightful stories have been related regarding this monster. Often when great storms raged at sea, sacrifices were made to him to appease his anger, for the Indians imagined he was the one that caused the disturbance. A dog would be killed and thrown into the lake, with the words, "Here is something for you, O Manitou; now be still and stop troubling the water."

According to the legend, this manitou was once a human being like all the other inhabitants of the village; in fact, he was the son of a great hunter named Ma-gee-we-non, and was his father's joy and pride. With the greatest delight the old warrior spent most of his time teaching his boy to shoot the arrow and throw the spear, and making him acquainted with all the knowledge necessary for an Indian brave's education. But in spite of all that was done to make the young man a great chief, he early evinced traits of a diabolical character. Although an adept in the use of his weapons, it became apparent that he was possessed of an evil spirit. He grew to large and ungainly proportions and became in truth a human monstrosity. He delighted in torturing people and did all sorts of things to annoy those about him. One day, highly incensed over his ill luck at fishing, he sought the feeding grounds of a dreaded sea-serpent, which he captured and turned loose in the village, where the enraged reptile killed many of the inhabitants and committed all sorts of depredations.

At this period the tribe was ruled over by a remark-able chieftain who was said to possess supernatural pow-ers. The Great Spirit had blessed him with an extremely beautiful daughter whose hand was sought by all the young braves of the surrounding country, among whom was Neoma, considered the best warrior and hunter in the tribe.

Wa-wass-ko-na (flower), the chief's daughter, returned the young man's affections, but Neoma had a rival in the powerful Motchi Manitou, and strange to say, the chief wished his daughter to marry the latter, hoping thereby to gain more power and influence and become greater than any of his predecessors.

Neoma asked the chief for his daughter's hand, but was, of course, rejected, and Wa-wass-ko-na was impris-oned in a separate wigwam, with guards placed at the en-trance, so that the lovers might not elope. But "love laughs at locksmiths," and one dark night Neoma stole into his

MOONLIGHT AT L'ARBRE CROCHE (Middle Village)

OLD CHURCH AND HOME OF THE PRIEST—Harbor Springs, 1842.

Photo by Troup

L'ARBRE CROCHE MISSION AS IT WAS 100 YEARS LATER

LOVER'S LANE
Section of an Old Indian Trail at Roaring Brook

GATHERING OF THE TRIBES AT WA-YA-GA-MUG

A SYLVAN PATH AT CHARLEVOIX

ISLAND IN GRAND TRAVERSE BAY

The scenery of Grand Traverse as well as Little Travers Bay is delightful

OLD RIVER
A Secluded Retreat at Charlevoix the Beautiful

CATHOLIC CHUCH AT MIDDLE VILLAGE

WHERE THE INDIAN DRUM BEATS AT L'ARBRE CROCHE

PRINCESS MARGARET BOYD
Sister of Chief Blackbird and benefactress of her race

NEGONEE, 106 YEARS OLD

This aged woman walked from the Indian village at Burt Lake, when it was burned by order of the sheriff, to Middle Village, where she soon after died. The despoliation and dispersion of the Burt Lake Indians forms one of the darkest pages of American history and proves the utter failure and weakness of the government's Indian policy in the past.

TOM SHOMIN, "ARROW MAKER"

A Cross Village Indian, eighty years old.

Photo by Foley
CHIEF IGNATIUS PETOSKEY, AFTER WHOM THE CITY
OF PETOSKEY WAS NAMED, WITH HIS TWO SONS,
LOUIS *(left)* AND ENOS *(right)* IN ENTRANCE OF
BAZILE PETOSKEY'S STORE 1878

INDIAN CEMETERY AT CROSS VILLAGE

This burial ground is so old some of the graves are found to be located one above the other

CHIEF BLACKBIRD

Who wrote an Ottawa grammar and history of his people

sweetheart's prison, first drugging the guards with a potion he had obtained from an old woman who resided in
the outskirts of the village. Wa-wass-ko-na was only too
glad to regain her freedom and join her faithful lover. They
hastily embarked in a canoe which Neoma had provided
for the occasion, and fled to an island far out in Lake Michigan (Manitou Island), where they landed, pitched their tent,
and for a time lived happily together.

But Motchi Manitou soon learned their whereabouts,
and one day when Neoma was away in quest of game,
hied himself to his wigwam and abducted his bride, whom
he carried to his abode—a desolate cave near the shore—
where he imprisoned her.

Neoma returned home, and missing his wife, spent
many weary hours of anguish, but at last surmised the cause
of her disappearance. He immediately started in pursuit of
Motchi Manitou, but arrived at the latter's rendezvous too
late to rescue Wa-wass-ko-na and was only met by the jeers
and mocking laughter of the Motchi Manitou. With a heavy
heart he lingered about the prison, contriving many plans
by which he might rescue his wife, but failed in all his
attempts.

Meanwhile Wa-wass-ko-na became heart-broken and
despondent and shed many tears. She rapidly failed in
health until she was only a mere skeleton of her former
self, and in a short time she crossed "the dark river of
death."

Neoma was overwhelmed with grief, and disheartened, he climbed "the crooked tree," which was not far from the Motchi Manitou's cave, and with a weird, plaintive death-song threw himself to the beach, striking in the waters of Lake Michigan, which caught up the sad air and have ever murmured the lament of the departed warrior.

At last the great Chieftain, Wa-was-ko-na's father, passed away and the people saw that in order to insure their safety, they must destroy the Motchi Manitou. A great council was held and it was decided that all the warriors should turn out en masse, to get him, dead or alive. But of no avail. He seemed to possess a charmed life. He never could be seen, but each morning the inhabitants of L'Arbre Croche would awaken to find new mischief or depredations.

Finally, after many days of searching, he was discovered, nestled among the sand dunes on the shore, fast asleep. Without losing any time the bravest of the people crept up cautiously and deftly bound him with basswood bark, so that when he awoke he was helpless. His captors then placed him in a canoe and, taking him far out into the bay, tied huge stones to his neck and threw him overboard. As he reached the water, by his exertions to get loose, he caused such a sea that the canoe was upset and all its occupants drowned.

Even to the present day, when great tempests rage on Lake Michigan, the older Indians say: "It's Motchi Manitou trying to get out of the water."

THE TREATY PAYMENT

In accordance with the terms of several treaties, the government made a number of annual payments to the Indians of L'Arbre Croche. Most of these payments were in merchandise, but the Indians also received large amounts of money, and some time previous to the arrival of the government agent, traders from all parts of the upper lake region would assemble with small stocks of goods to traffic with the natives.

Glancing for a moment at the scene of one of these government treaty payments, we see a vast and varied concourse of people. Along the shore as far as the eye can reach are numerous small tents, huddled together as close as it is convenient to pitch them—the temporary abode of those Indians coming from a distance. Large crowds of Ottawas, painted and bedecked with feathers, and wearing the native costumes, stand upon every corner, while many whites intermingle with their dusky brethren and dart hither and thither in apparent confusion. From the narrow wharf near the center of the village we push our way along with the rabble, for such it may be called, and soon find themselves in front of the old government building at the foot of the bluff, where we are informed the payments will begin at 1 o'clock sharp. We wait, for the time is near at hand, and presently the doors of the old building are thrown open and a rush is made by the Indians to get inside, each anxious to receive his annuity first. Door tenders, however, keep them back and an interpreter gives the information that only one chief with his band is to come in at a time, the one with the largest following to be first, and so on.

The first chief, or headman, with about 100 followers, enters and is marched up to the farther end of the large room, where he is obliged to certify before the Indian agent that all the persons with him are lawful members of his band. The headman then signs his name, or makes his mark, to the effect that he has received the amount due him from the great white father.

This ceremony over, the Indians repair to a long counter on one side of the room where numerous clerks are stationed to wait upon them. Each Indian and squaw is given so many blankets, a number of yards of different kinds of cloth, cooking utensils, provisions, etc., and a number of farm implements to promote agriculture amongst them; and in addition to this the men are each allowed a quantity of tobacco. Lastly comes the specie payment. This is done under the direct supervision of the Indian agent, and the Indians hold their blankets to catch the glittering gold and silver. After the payment the Indians withdraw to the street with smiles of satisfaction.

And now comes the turn of the traders, who, in many cases, soon have the Indians under the control of their fire

water, and a system of cheating, thievery and knavery pre-
vails which can be perpetrated only upon unsophisticated
savages.

Through curiosity we enter one of the little stores near
at hand to see the Indians do their trading. One, who has
received his annuity, is passing along when his squaw spies
a bright colored shawl and immediately she wishes to purchase it. They come in and point to the shawl, and the
proprietor, who is perfectly familiar with their mode of
shopping, takes it down and by his energetic talk and dis-
play of goods, induces them to purchase it and numerous
other articles besides. When their selections are made, the
Indian takes his blanket from his shoulders, unties the cor-
ners and spreads his money out upon the counter. He is
unable to count it, so the trader "rakes in" what he deems
sufficient pay for his goods, with no stint as to profit, and
the Indian ties up the rest and with his squaw goes out to
visit some other store.

Sometimes several days were consumed in the payment of the different bands, after which the traders and
Indians packed up and left for their respective homes—
not a vestige remaining of the erstwhile populous village
along the shore.

The Indians of L'Arbre Croche have always believed
that considerable money still remained to their credit in
Washington. No doubt they never received all that the government promised or intended that they should. In some
cases dishonest agents were probably the cause. It is re-

lated that one agent, who was sent to the Indians with thirty thousand dollars for specie payments, secured the signatures of the headmen and then disbursed only ten thousand.

So, during the administration of Grover Cleveland, an Indian by the name of Shawn succeeded in collecting enough money by subscription to take himself and a number of companions to Washington to look into the matter and see if they could not collect what they claimed was still due in the way of interest and unpaid treaty money.

They did not succeed in their enterprise, but were well received and royally entertained at the capital. They stayed until their money was all gone and finally a collection had to be taken up to get them back home.

When they returned to L'Arbre Croche a great feast was being held at which Shawn related his experience.

THE GREAT FEAST OF THE OTTAWAS

The great feast of the Ottawa Indians at L'Arbre Croche during the days of its final glory was called Tu-san-wung, which annually took place on the eve of All Saints' day. It was the outgrowth of a barbarous custom the wild Indians had for remembering their dead, mixed with some of the civilized forms of more modern times. When the early missionaries first came to this country they saw the futility of trying to induce the Indians to at once give up their wild demonstration of grief over their departed people, so a sort of compromise was made by uniting it with the church's celebration of All Saints' day, in French, *Tout Saints* (hence the Indian term Tu-san-wung), at which the participants continued in a measure some of their strange and superstitious ceremonies, one being that of "Shooting the Devil" and another "Feeding the Dead."

When the repast was about half over, all present would repair to some high eminence and build a fire, around which they would dance and shout at the top of their voices; occasionally the men would go to the edge of the hill and shoot volleys up into the air, with the words, "amo awda"—"let us drive him away," referring to the evil spirit. After the atmosphere was thought to be cleared, the natives would go back and finish their feast.

Those who gave it invited, besides others, one person for each dead relative they had. These especially favored ones were supposed to personify the departed relatives, and the more they ate the better were the host and hostess pleased. Food was also placed on the graves, and if in a few days it had disappeared, it was a token that the dead were pleased and had eaten it; if it still remained at the end of a certain period, it was said that the spirits were angry and another feast would have to be given to satisfy them. The one who found a bean or a small coin that was previously placed in cookies that were passed at the table, would be the one to give the next feast.

It was near the close of one of these feasts when the weird ceremonies attending the "shooting of the devil" and the "feeding of the dead" had been performed, that Shawn, the Indian who had been to Washington, was invited to address the assembled guests and tell them about his wonderful trip. He responded in English as follows:

"We come on Washington. Beeg crowd. Band play. Musick. March. Go to hotel. Have ice cream, cake, pie, good nice eating. Bimeby go on White House. Knock. Mr. Washington come to door. When he see us he say, 'Beesy, come tomollow.'

"Tomollow we come again to White House. Knock. Mr. Washington come to door. He say, 'Beesy, come tomollow.'

"Tomollow we come again to White House. Knock.

Mr. Washington say, 'Come in.' He say, 'What's matter?'

"Mr. Washington tike down beeg book. Turn over. Turn over. Turn over. Turn over. Bimeby he say, 'Sorry. Too bad. No money here for Injun.'

"I say. You take much land—you owe Injun money.'

"Mr. Washington say, 'I buy land, give Money, got receipt.'"

"'No mistake,' say Mr. Washington. 'Let Injun hunt, fish.'

"'Land, all gone. No more hunt. Can't catch 'em fish.'

"'I tell you,' say Mr. Washington, 'be good Injun, pray, go to church, don't bother white man, bimeby die, go to heaven.'

"I reply, 'My friend, I'm 'fraid you make great mistake. White man can't get in heaven; how can Injun do it? Impossible.'"

Though Shawn did not accomplish much at Washington, his speech created considerable enthusiasm at home.

OUTWITTING A WHITE MAN

After the lands that were secured by the government through treaties with the Indians were thrown open for general settlement, many white people flocked to L'Arbre Croche from all parts of the country. The Indians were given first choice in selecting homesteads, and consequently in most cases held the best pieces of land. These homesteads were looked upon with envious eyes by the more rapacious of the white settlers and became common prey for the land sharks, who frequently secured the choicest farms for little or no consideration.

The Indians, unused to property ownership by deed, and not understanding the system of taxation inaugurated by the whites, often neglected to pay their assessments, and tax titles were thus easily obtained by unscrupulous parties who would seize the property and eject the original owners at the first opportunity. An Indian could not understand how a little piece of paper with his signature, or more often only his mark upon it, could be so valuable as to allow the one who held it to take away his home. All the business transactions ever carried on among the natives while they retained their tribal relations were made by word of mouth; the Indian valued his word and would keep it under all circumstances. A signature could mean little to him unless accompanied by a verbal promise. Lying was an unknown art among the red men. Not so with the whites. The latter made many promises which they failed to keep; as the Indians kept theirs, the advantage was always on the other side. When they were compelled to leave their property and were forcibly removed, they looked upon the transaction as little better than simple robbery.

By such actions on the part of the land sharks, the Indians were gradually pushed farther and farther towards the interior of the country, but in time some of them learned in a measure the ways of their white brothers, and were therefore enabled occasionally to drive a bargain whereby they secured something near what their farms or lots were worth.

The Indian settlement was surveyed and platted into a village by the government, and a certain prominent white man secured one of the lots by the payment of a very small sum of money. A number of years afterwards, upon examination, by a prospective buyer, it was found that the deed was faulty, and that it would be necessary to have a certain male heir who lived in another town, and his wife, sign it.

The white man therefore hired an interpreter to go with him to the town where the heirs resided, to secure their signatures. After considerable time in hunting him up and locating him, the Indian, whose name was Chokun, agreed that he and his wife would sign the deed for $25. The white man tried to argue him into reducing the amount, but the

Indian was obdurate, claiming that he had suffered much at the hands of the whites, and he and his wife wouldn't think of signing their names for any less amount. He spoke very good English, it was found, and made a grand plea for his people. At last the white man said he would pay the sum demanded, and secretly told his interpreter that he was glad to get off at that. So Chokun sent for his wife, a very comely squaw, and the party repaired to the office of a justice of the peace. After the papers were made out, the white man told Chokun to sign his name.

"Give me twenty-five dollars," said Chokun.

"Oh, certainly," replied the other, handing him the money.

Chokun took the proffered pen, signed his name and stepped aside.

"Now have your wife sign it," said the white man, all smiles.

Chokun turned to his wife and a few words were spoken by them in Indian. As the woman made no move to put down her name, the white man asked:

"What does she say?"

"My wife say he want twenty-five dollars, too," said Chokun.

"Oh, no," exclaimed the white man, "you agreed to both sign for that sum and you can't get any more out of me.

The woman remained stationary.

"My wife he want twenty-five dollars, too," repeated Chokun.

"Come," said the white man; "you can't work that kind of a game. Have your wife sign the deed and hurry up."

There was silence for several moments.

"My wife he want twenty-five dollars, too," again repeated Chokun, firmly.

The white man was flushed with anger and paced the floor nervously. No amount of argument could make the Indians change their minds, so he finally opened his pocketbook and gave Mrs. Chokun the required $25 and forthwith she signed her name.

This is probably about one case in a thousand where an Indian got the better of a bargain when dealing with a white man.

THE FLIGHT OF "RISING SUN"

As far as historians have been able to ascertain, all pagan Indians believed in the immortality of the soul. The Algonquin tribes generally and the Ottawas in particular thought that there was a broad, beautiful prairie, lying at a great distance, abounding in the finest game of all kinds where the warrior went after death to feast, dance and revel in happiness forever and ever. The road to this happy hunting ground, called Ke-wa-kun-ah, "homeward road," or Che-ba-kun-ah, "ghost road," was said to be so difficult of passage that no mortal could ever hope to pass over it; indeed it was only the bravest souls even after death that ever reached the Indian's heaven; the weakest, including women and children, falling by the wayside. It was discovered and revealed to the people by a great warrior, who, in a trance, traveled over the "road of the dead," followed by his mother and sweetheart. Being assisted by kindly spirits, the former finally captured him, and brought him back to the land of the living to tell his wonderful story.

Long before the paleface had ventured upon the Indian's native land there dwelt upon the banks of Lake Michigan, near the resort now called We-que-ton-sing, a squaw upwards of four score years of age, who went by the name of No-ko-qua. Her husband, who was a great chieftain in his day, had passed to the great beyond, but he had left a son, who like himself, was the wonder and pride of the whole tribe. He excelled in the chase; as a runner he could not be beaten, and in battle he always secured the most scalps. His name was Pe-tos-key, which means "the rising sun." The companions of Petoskey had no chance to win any prizes when he entered the lists; his arrow always flew the straightest; his eye could see the farthest; and his strength was so great that he could attack the most ferocious animals empty-handed and come off victorious.

One night, after returning from a hunt in which he had been unusually successful, Petoskey was suddenly stricken with a strange malady, and before dawn he lay unconscious upon his couch of skins. There was much sorrow throughout the village and requiem songs and laments could be heard in every wigwam. For many days the chief remained in a comatose condition, his aged mother, No-ko-qua, and also his sweetheart, Winona, who was the most beautiful maiden among the Ottawas, being constantly at his bedside, until they, too, from sheer exhaustion, were compelled to lie down.

Suddenly they were awakened by a blood-curdling war whoop, which echoed loudly through the still night air. No-ko-qua and Winona jumped to their feet, and as they did so, beheld Petoskey arisen from his bed, arrayed in all the paraphernalia of war, but before they could catch hold of him he uttered another piercing cry and bounded out of the door. Thinking he had left his bed in a delirium, they started in pursuit.

"Pe-tos-key! Pe-tos-key!" cried the women, but Pe-toskey paid no attention to their entreaties, running only the faster.

Then Winona, with girlish fickleness, gave up the chase and returned to her father's wigwam; not so No-ko-qua, whose mother-love was a surpassing virtue. With a doggedness born of despair she clung to the trail, which was doubly difficult to do because Petoskey no longer ran upon the ground but a little distance up in the air.

Then she realized that she was upon the che-ba-kun-ah, or "ghost road," but determined to continue her pursuit, because she was satisfied that her son was still alive. All the rest of that night she followed him as best she could, sur-mounting the most annoying obstacles. Finally she came to a broad river, gee-ba-ya ze-ba, "the river of death," in which a large splashing tree indicated to all departed spirits the place to cross. The river appeared like a huge serpent, for-ever twisting and crawling. A little distance away she saw a wigwam, and going thither she knocked at the door. An old man made his appearance, who in great surprise asked her what she wanted.

"You are on the road of the dead," said he, "why are you wandering in this direction?"

"Have you seen my son, Petoskey, the great warrior and chieftain?" asked No-ko-qua.

"Yes," replied the old man, "he passed over the river a

short time ago. But I fear you cannot follow him. It is a dangerous and difficult thing and you are sure to fall in the water. I am stationed here by Gitchi Manitou to brain all people who may pass this way, so they can forget their worldly troubles and forever enjoy themselves in the Happy Hunting Grounds which lie at the end of the road. But they must first register their entry into the realm of death by tasting of the fruit of life which lies yonder. Your son was unable to do this, so I did not remove his brains; he is not dead but travels in a trance."

Looking to the place indicated by the old man, No-ko-qua saw a huge strawberry covered with tooth-marks made by departed warriors. As the braves stooped over to take a bite of the berry, the guardsman brained them with a sharp, quick blow from his tomahawk, and the severed organ was thrown into a mow-cock, or birch-bark box.

Without losing any time, No-ko-qua attempted to cross the river by crawling along the tree. She had not proceeded far, however, until she slipped and fell into the dark, angry waters. Calling for assistance, she again attracted the old guardsman, who came and pulled her out. Beneath her she noticed many minnows swimming about in all directions. These, the guardsman assured her, were the spirits of little children and those who struggled to cross the river but could not do so and finally fell into the water.

In response to her many entreaties the guardsman at last assisted her across to the other shore, and again she started on Petoskey's trail.

Before long she came to a steep mountain over which it was impossible to pass. In vain she searched for a breach or opening of some sort so that she might make her way to the other side, and was about to give up in despair when she espied that terrible passageway, where two pestles of prodigious size rise and fall alternately. There is room for but a single person to enter and the soul must dodge quickly, first under one and then under the other, in order to pass in safety. Many get caught and perish, especially the weak and aged, but No-ko-qua after watching the proceedings for some time, boldly made the attempt and succeeded in slipping unharmed underneath the pestles.

She then found herself in a most beautiful country. There were all kinds of fruits in abundance and flowers were blooming on every hand. The roadway of the dead led on through this delightful country to a grand forest in which songbirds of all kinds were flooding the air with wonderful melodies.

No-ko-qua followed her son for two days more, and on the third, just as the sun was sinking, she arrived at the edge of a large clearing from which proceeded the songs and laughter of a large multitude.

She had reached the Happy Hunting Grounds. Seeing a little wigwam near by, she knocked at the doorpost and was admitted by a squaw as old as herself, who said she, too, had followed a son under similar circumstances; and although he came every night to hunt and dance and enjoy himself in the beautiful clearing she could not capture him for he was really dead. She bade her guest remain with her a little while, when she promised to point out Petoskey, for she had seen him the night before.

They waited together outside the tent, and just as the moon showed its silvery beams, an old man came and seated himself in the center of the field and dark shadows glided into the opening, dancing and shouting to the music of his tom-tom. Deer, elk, buffalos and bears and all kinds of game mingled with the happy warriors. Occasionally one of the shades would cautiously approach to the place where the old women were watching, and pointing his finger at them would say, "Look at the live people—how funny they are. Go on home and leave us here in happiness. All the live people are foolish and we don't want to be bothered with them any more," then laughing gayly would run away to again join in the sport of his fellows.

One of the last to enter the field was a young brave who did not seem to enjoy himself like the others, but kept clasping his hands to his head and crying, "My head is heavy! Oh, my head is so heavy!"

This, No-ko-qua recognized as her son, Petoskey, whose distress was caused by his brains, which the old man stationed at the river of death had been unable to remove, because he was not dead.

The women waited until he staggered toward them and as he did so, they grasped him tightly and stuffed him into a sack, which had been provided for the occasion, so that he could not escape. Then taking him to the wigwam they put him through a series of sweats, produced by hot stones and sand, and the young man was soon brought back to consciousness.

No-ko-qua and her son remained with their kind hostess for some time after his resuscitation, watching the festivities of the dead each night, but as they were unable to share in their happiness, they soon began their perilous journey back to the land of the living, where they arrived in due time. They were received with open arms, and the union of Petoskey and Winona was solemnized at a great feast where the young hero related to a breathless multitude his experience in the Happy Hunting Grounds.

The Ottawas of L'Arbre Croche still cherish many superstitions based on this tradition. They regard the strawberry with the greatest reverence, since the legend says it is the fruit of life; and they never kill little minnows because their fathers taught that they were the souls of departed children.

THE GREAT FIGHT BETWEEN THE CLANS

It is not generally understood why the missions were practically abandoned for many years, but a reliable tradition informs us that the abandonment was due to a terrible massacre, which took place at the most northern part of L'Arbre Croche, now known as Cross Village.

A new church had been built there, and the Reverend Father du Jaunay was planning an imposing ceremony on the feast of All Saints' day. Accordingly a large concourse of people gathered and the village was in gala attire; warriors bedecked with paint and feathers were present from all parts of the country, promenading through the little streets, or sitting in groups on the brow of the bluff smoking their calumets and relating stories. The clans of the Turtle, the Eagle and the Beaver were more in evidence than others, and could be recognized by the elaborate emblems they wore and by their proud and haughty bearing.

The day before the priest arrived the village was filled with eager people and the beach as far as the eye could reach was literally covered with tents and wigwams. Towards evening many camp fires were lighted and the curling smoke bespoke the great feast on the morrow when the beloved pale face Father would be present to tell them of a wonderful Redeemer who was said to love the Indian as much as the white man and who had died to save all mankind. Foot races, target shooting and quash-go-na-win (jumping) contests had been indulged in throughout the day and the most weary of the athletes were preparing to retire for the night.

A maiden of the Turtle clan was walking along the shore a short distance front her tent. A young brave, wearing the totem of the Beaver, crept up cautiously behind her. As she stooped to dip some water in her birchen pail, he sprang forward and seized her, and attempted to drag her toward the forest, holding one hand tightly over her mouth. But he had overestimated his strength; moreover he was wild and excited from several draughts of a peculiar beverage he had obtained from a trader, which he called sko-da-wa-bo, "fire water." He staggered and his foot slipped.

The maiden, with the agility of a tigress, sprang from his grasp, and uttered the war-cry of the Turtles. Immediately a dozen brawny forms were at her side. She displayed her torn garments and pointed to the Beaver, who was trying to escape in the bushes. They at once swooped upon him, their tomahawks gleaming in the air. Seeing his approaching doom, he, in turn, raised the war cry of his clan. A moment later his form lay stark and bleeding on the ground, and his scalp-lock was handed to the maiden whom he had attacked.

According to the information, it is a calm autumn night; the moon is shining brightly overhead, and everyone is living in joyous expectation of the coming fete. Suddenly two blood curdling war-whoops rend the air. The people immediately jump to their feet and pandemonium is let loose. Lamentations, shouts and wails betoken the ire of the Beavers. There is no time for a council, at which the judgment of the wiser men might prevent further bloodshed; neither is there any precious moment lost in war dances or other preparations. Instead, the infuriated Beavers single out their new-made enemies, and a hand-to-hand combat ensues with frightful results. Here, a fallen brave writhes in agony upon the ground, his skull sunken by the stone hatchet of his adversary who wields his weapon with unerring aim; yonder, a young mother weeps over the mangled form of her husband, while a score of murdered bodies strew the ground in all directions. A lad who tries to recover his father's belongings, after the latter has been slain, is seized by the ankles and his head dashed against a tree; a frenzied demon has severed the head of a victim from its body, and grasping it by the hair, swings it several times above his head, throwing it with terrific force against a projecting rock; the shouting and yelling are deafening and the carnage continues until the soil is drenched with blood. Finally the chieftain of the Eagles, who have had no part in the affair, sides with the Turtles, and puts an end to the bloody tragedy. Not, however, until the Beavers are all but exterminated.

The morning sun rises bright and clear and reveals a calamity appalling in its desolation and destruction.

A little canoe is seen approaching in the distance, bearing the aged missionary and his two Indian escorts. Arriving upon the scene of the massacre, it is said, he raised his hands on high and exclaimed: "The earth bleeds and heaven weeps! Oh, what have my poor children done? Never can I set foot in this place again. I have labored zealously, but can do nothing."

What was to have been a wonderful Christian demonstration was thus transformed into a pitiful scene of sorrow and distress. Packing up his few belongings, the good Father du Jaunay left the country, nevermore to return.

The log structure he used at L'Arbre Croche, and which answered the purposes of a church for many years, at last passed into decay. Another more commodious structure was then constructed, which in turn gave way to another, to be occasionally visited by missionaries, but the Indian population has dwindled until only a few remain.

LAST OF THE CHIEFS

Blackbird was the last hereditary chief of the Ottawas of L'Arbre Croche. He and his sister, Margaret Boyd, the latter known as the Indian princess, were both well educated and did much for the advancement of their people. Chief Blackbird wrote a short history of the Ottawas and a grammar of their language; he also gave lectures, and recited original compositions, which attracted widespread attention. His sister, Margaret, once went to Washington and was granted an audience by President Garfield. Blackbird and his sister possessed more than ordinary ability. They were kind and good to the poor, and both deplored to the last the encroachment of the whites.

Blackbird's predecessor was Ne-se-wa-quat, or Chief Fork-in-the-Tree, whose father was acting chief at the time the Ottawas gave up their tribal relations and became citizens of the United States.

Chief Fork-in-the-Tree had a son who got into some kind of trouble and as a result was sent to the Detroit House of Correction while his father was still living. This greatly worried the old warrior, who lamented continually for his boy. One day he met an acquaintance whom he asked for a bowl of tobacco, and having received it, he commenced to tell how badly he felt for his son in prison.

"Oh, don't worry for him," said his friend. "He's all right where he is."

"But he must be very poorly fed and ill-treated," said the old chief sorrowfully.

"Oh, not at all," replied the other. "On the contrary, he has his meals brought to him regularly, has a good place to sleep, and a steady job."

"Is that possible?" exclaimed Fork-in-the-Tree.

"Yes, sir," continued the other, "and besides that they even give him a certain allowance of good tobacco (Samaw)."

The old Indian laughed. "By golly!" he said. "Me like to go there, too."

THE STRANGE CASE OF DR. WEIKAMP

About the middle of the last century there arrived at
L'Arbre Croche a small Mackinaw sailboat carrying a
Catholic priest and a few brothers and sisters of the order
of St. Francis. The priest informed the villagers that he
came to make his home in that part of the country and
intended to establish a convent somewhere in the neighborhood; he had lately been at the head of a similar in-
stitution which he had founded in Chicago in conjunction
with a wealthy woman who came with him from Germany,
his native land; but his building having been mysteriously
set on fire and destroyed, he had decided to labor among
the Indians. After looking over the ground, he purchased a
tract of two thousand acres, located at a point called Cross
Village; and shortly afterwards he and his followers began
the construction of a large wooden edifice thereafter known
as the Cross Village Convent. Father Weikamp was a tertiary Franciscan, or monk of the third degree, and being
unable to secure the necessary permission from his superi-
ors, he acted on his own initiative in this manner. The or-
ganization he established was entitled the Benevolent,
Charitable and Religious Society of St. Francis, in honor
of his patron saint.

Father Weikamp soon proved to be a very odd and eccentric character, and besides a convent, hospital and other buildings, he also had constructed a sepulchre which he kept in readiness to receive his remains whenever the time came for him to lay aside his earthly cares. This sepulchre consisted of a deep cellar, well walled, covered by a small building that stood perhaps six or eight feet above the ground. The structure was located at some distance from the convent, to the right, in the open field, and was always kept securely locked. No one aside from the tertiary and a few intimate friends knew exactly what the sepulchre contained. There was known to be a casket in the center of the cellar, surmounted by a skull and cross bones, beside which the priest daily made three hours of meditation; and frequently he went to the gruesome place to read books and papers or for his after dinner smoke, of which he was said to be very fond.

Divers were the stories related of the good monk and the secrets of his "private cellar," as some of the villagers persisted in calling the sepulchre. Some claimed it was filled with casks of choice wine, while others declared it to be the rendezvous of the wealthy woman from Germany.

Regardless of this gossip, Father Weikamp kept the even tenor of his way, going on calls to the sick when needed, and attending to his regular duties at the church.

For many years the society thrived, land was cleared, a grist mill, saw mill and shops were erected, besides a parochial school for Indian children. The brothers proved excellent farmers and the crops and stock they raised made the convent self-supporting.

All the years the colony was in existence Father Weikamp could be seen each day going to the sepulchre, from which he would usually return to the convent from three to four hours later. If anyone called for him during the hours of his meditation, his strict orders were that he should not be disturbed. His visits to the sepulchre became so regular and of such common occurrence that finally they ceased to cause any comment.

As the monk advanced in years his meditations were prolonged, and at last he called his associates about him and gave them instructions regarding his burial, for he now felt that he had not long to remain among them.

A few days later, while returning from a drive through the country, his horse became frightened, and in the runaway that ensued Father Weikamp received internal injuries from which he did not recover.

A friend who had long known him, upon hearing of his serious illness, hastened to Cross Village from a distant town to be at his bedside, if possible, before dissolution should take place. The friend, however, arrived belated; in fact he did not reach the convent until Father Weikamp had been laid to rest in the sepulchre. But this he did not know until later. He claims to have seen the tertiary upon his arrival that night, alive and well, three days after his death and once after his burial, according to the records. Regarding the occurrence he tells a story almost beyond belief. Did we not know him to be a man of sterling qualities and utmost reliability, we might doubt his word. As it is, we can only marvel, and enter the incident on the list of unexpected phenomena that baffles the mind of man. Our informant's name we are not at this time at liberty to disclose, but his remarkable story in his own words is as follows:

"Father Weikamp and I had been, since our acquaintance a few months after his arrival at Cross Village, on very intimate terms. I felt considerable pride, I must acknowledge, in knowing that I was one of the few in whom he seemed to have real confidence. He often invited me to the convent and even asked me upon several occasions to accompany him to his sepulchre or underground vault. I always gladly accepted these invitations, partly at first, I will admit, from curiosity; but also on account of genuine friendship. While in the little room upon my last visit I remember distinctly Father Weikamp telling me of his firm conviction and belief in a future life. He was rather eloquent in his statements and I was struck with his sincerity. We conversed at length upon the subject, and as I was about to go, I suggested to him that whichever one of us should die first would, if within his power, manifest himself to the other in some manner. He readily consented to this proposition and seemed pleased with the idea.

"When I learned of his last illness I was at a distant point on urgent business, but started immediately for his bedside to see him once more if possible before he passed away. After a long ride, I reached the convent late at night and in order not to cause any undue disturbance, I decided to hitch my horse temporarily while I went to the door to find out whether I had arrived too late or was yet in time to see my friend. I remembered that a little distance beyond the convent, in the direction I was traveling, there was a little sheltered arbor and hitching post beside the roadway where I had sought refuge once before, and in going thither I glanced toward the sepulchre which was now within my view. To my astonishment I saw a light issuing therefrom. As soon as I reached the arbor I hitched my horse hurriedly, and started across lots towards the sepulchre, to see what was taking place at that late hour. As I neared the little building, I could distinctly hear Father Weikamp's voice alternately singing and praying. The door was flung wide open and looking in I beheld him on his knees as I had seen him many times before. I could not have been mistaken—I was too well acquainted with that short, rotund figure, and full, red face surmounted by a fringe of white. I, of course, concluded that he had recovered from his illness and not wishing to disturb him, quietly withdrew to the convent, where I knocked at the door and was admitted by one of his sisters of the society. I told her I had come hurriedly from a distance to see Father Weikamp knowing that he had been very ill; but was glad to see that he had recovered.

"'Indeed,' said she, 'the good Father died several days ago and was laid to rest in his sepulchre yesterday.'

"'Impossible!' I exclaimed; 'I was just there and saw him kneeling in front of his coffin as usual.'

"'We will go and see if any strange thing has taken place,'" said the nun, who called another, and accompanied by the two I returned to the sepulchre.

"When we arrived there all was dark; the tomb was securely locked, with absolutely no signs of any living thing within. To satisfy my curiosity the sister, who remembered me well as a friend of Father Weikamp, unlocked the door and we entered with a lighted lantern. All was still as death and everything in its proper place. The lid of the coffin containing Father Weikamp's remains was firmly fastened and appeared to have been neither moved nor molested. We opened the casket, to more thoroughly convince ourselves regarding the matter, and beheld the familiar features of the dead tertiary, whose body was in precisely the same position in which it had been placed the day before by the members of the Benevolent, Charitable and Religious Society of St. Francis."

LEGEND OF THE MOUNDS

A few miles north of L'Arbre Croche, beneath the wide-spreading boughs of a large oak, are two mounds whose history reveals a pathetic story of love and tragedy.

During the palmy days of the Ottawas of this region, when their arrows brought the crimson blood spouting forth from the fleet-footed deer and their war-whoops sent terror to the hearts of the braves of all contemporary tribes, Weosma, a noted warrior and hunter, whose aim was perfect and whose foot was as light as a roe's, resided with his aged mother in the village of a renowned clan to the north.

Each young maiden of the neighborhood, it is said, had fond hopes that sooner or later her charms would attract the young man's attention, but he was heedless to all such allurements, until one day the nymph of love made her appearance and Weosma became a victim as helpless as any ever was before.

His inamorata was Enewah, the bewitching daughter of the great chief who ruled over the destiny of his people at that time. Weosma had first met her while on a hunting expedition in the south, and ever after that eventful day his life was not the same; he was unhappy when out of her company and seemed to take pleasure only in performing brave deeds that he might be worthy of Enewah's love. She in turn looked with favor upon his attentions and ere long the necessary parental consent was obtained and a date announced for the wedding ceremony. Great reparations were made for the occasion, and all looked bright and promising for the future life of the young couple.

But in the annals of L'Arbre Croche, as elsewhere, the course of true love never did run smooth, and an evil one appeared upon the scene, who, by the fertility of a cunning brain, blasted forever the high hopes and fond dreams of the devoted pair. Amo, the Bee, a rejected suitor of Enewah's, had sworn revenge upon the fair young maiden, and now came a glorious opportunity to carry out the vendetta.

As Weosma was a very popular young man, it was decided to hold a great feast in honor of his success in winning the chieftain's daughter. The evening previous to the occasion Amo arrived at Enewah's wigwam in breathless haste and warned the young girl not to marry a man who was already betrothed to a woman of another tribe, which, to the Ottawas, was a terrible crime. Enewah only laughed in scorn at the Bee's scheme and turned away, saying that Weosma was too good a man to do anything of that kind. Then Amo told the story to her father, the great chief, who, thinking him his friend, forbade his daughter marrying such a scoundrel as Weosma was shown to be.

When therefore Weosma arrived at Enewah's wigwam that evening to present her with a white deer skin that he had just taken, the chief received him very coldly and told him what he had heard. Excuses were of no avail and after a few words Weosma was ordered out of his sight forever.

In despair the young man returned to his home. The next morning bright and early he took down his bow and quiver of arrows and started for the forest. He returned shortly, bringing with him two white pigeons, which he threw upon the ground before his mother, saying: "Mother, I am as innocent as these pigeons of the crime of which I am accused; I know you will believe me if no one else will. These are the last birds I will ever shoot for you," and as he uttered the words he drove his hunting knife to his heart and expired.

The news of his death spread quickly throughout the tribe, and the gay throng that was to gather en fête on the morrow was turned into one of utter chagrin and discouragement. The festive dances were abandoned and instead could be heard the mournful notes of the songs of lament.

When the chief heard of the story of the pigeons he at once summoned Amo, "The Bee," but the latter, thinking the truth would be discovered, had fled the country.

Enewah, who had cherished the hope that her lover might be proved innocent in the sight of her father, became almost frantic at the sad news of his death. She rapidly pined away, and finally ended her earthly existence in the same manner as Weosma, exclaiming: "Bama pe ning ga wa ba ma," which translated means, "I will see him by and by."

The two mounds mark the spot where the lovers were laid to rest side by side and the silent forest has kept the secret for more than a century.

THE GREAT MUCKWAH

Frequently we find more than one legend regarding a certain place. This is largely accounted for by the not uncommon custom of adopting stories of friendly tribes, which often passed current from one to the other. For example, the writer has beard at least three different legends as to the origin of Mackinac Island, all of which were authentic Indian stories. Following is another version of the Sleeping Bear:

From the land of the Illinois word came to the tribes of Michigan that a giant black bear had made its appearance and was killing many people and devastating the country. In vain had the boldest hunters essayed to match their strength and skill with that of the great "muckwah." It was said that he was so large and powerful that he paid no attention whatever to arrows or spears; but knocked over the strongest warriors with a mere slap of his huge paw and devoured men, women and children. All the country was in alarm and people fled from their homes to places of safety.

No calamity of equal importance had occurred since the great famine or the days of the flood.

Sogimaw, the most noted hunter of the Ottawas, was prevailed upon to seek the monster and slay him. Sogimaw was gone a fortnight and returned with the word that he had seen Muckwah; but if he were ten times as strong and as big as twenty more men like himself he would still be no match for the animal.

The people all shuddered at his story; and were further terror-stricken when the report came that the giant bear was making his way northward, leaving death and desolation in his wake. They huddled together in the wigwams, quaking with fear at every little noise, thinking it might be Muckwah ready to pounce upon them.

Mondapee, an old brave who towered head and shoulders above his companions—a veteran who had been able to overpower all his adversaries, laughed and said, "Do not be alarmed, my children; I will go forth and kill Muckwah."

With his heaviest warclub, arrayed in his famous fighting costume, Mondapee sallied forth amid the plaudits of his people. For six days nothing was heard from him; but horrible stories still reached his tribesmen regarding the predations of the great bear. So a searching party was sent out for the warrior. Not very far from his home in the forest, near a clump of hemlock trees, they found Mondapee's warclub and a few belongings. He had been torn to pieces and devoured by Muckwah.

A day or two later a little girl ran breathless into her parents' wigwam saying that she had seen Muckwah; that he had killed the two companions with whom she was playing, but by running swiftly through the bushes she herself bad managed to escape. When asked to describe the monster she said he was taller than the highest wigwam and longer than six canoes placed end to end.

Frantically the people hid themselves in caves and in other out of the way places. Any person who had the temerity to stray away to any distance generally disappeared forever; and if they were so fortunate as to return it was always with additional tales of rapine and murder.

Wily and crafty runners were sent out over the country in an effort to band the inhabitants together for a united attack upon Muckwah but before the plan could he put into execution the ferocious beast attacked three of the largest villages in the proposed federation and destroyed every wigwam. It seemed as though the monster was destined to crush all human opposition, and the population was in despair.

A few days after this cataclysm, however, it was reported that Muckwah, satiated with his crimes and misdemeanors, had curled up on the shore of the lake to take his long winter nap. Now was the time for action! Councils were held and vast bands of warriors assembled; huge flint-tipped arrows were hastily manufactured and giant spears devised; war dances were the common pastime, and soon the signal smoke arose from every hilltop.

In the meantime, while all these vast preparations were going on, Muckwah was overpowered and conquered; not by warriors, but by a gentle maiden, who to save the people, carried a potion from an old sorceress, and creeping cautiously over the sand dunes, placed it carefully at the nostrils of the bear. Muckwah was soon overcome by the powerful fumes and expired with scarcely a struggle.

He lies to this day where his death took place, on the east shore of Lake Michigan, where he may be seen from passing boats at a point called Sleeping Bear.

THE WISE CHIEFTAIN OF BAY VIEW

Ne-bwa Ka-o-ke-maw was a very learned Indian, his name signifying the wise chieftain. Most of his people resided on the north side of Little Traverse bay, but what is now Bay View, the summer city, seemed to have a strange fascination for him; and he built a house there which be named "Bay-she-kane-daw-kwuck ne wigwam," meaning "My beautiful home."

Often after he had returned from the chase, Ne-bwa Ka-o-ke-maw would sit on the shore near his wigwam and watch the setting sun, and after night had spread her sable folds he would meditate on the moon and stars. It is related to him that he composed poetry which he took great delight in reciting to his subjects.

The following stanza, which was handed down from generation to generation among the Indians, is said to have been composed by this wonderful man:

> Anawe awe waiabine wingwed
> Agimakang jajaie nindakimina;
> Aka dash wi wika odamakasin
> Wadashi minawanigo kioseiang.
> Translation:
> Although the cruel paleface
> In our land may now be found,
> He will never find a place
> In our happy hunting ground.

He was found dead one morning on the beach, where he had remained all night trying to make out what the stars were.

He was buried near the spot he loved so well, amid the sorrow of his entire tribe.

THE INDIAN COMPANY

A company of Indian soldiers from the Arbre Croche country fought in the Civil War under General Grant from the battle of the Wilderness until the surrender of the Confederates at Appomattox Court House. Company K, First Michigan Sharpshooters, was mustered into service January 1863; was stationed for a time at Fort Dearborn to guard the State arsenal at that place and soon after was ordered to the front. With Grant the Indians crossed the Rapidan and received their baptism of fire in the terrible battle of the Wilderness. They also took part in the hard-fought engagements of Spottsylvania Court House, Cold Harbor and Petersburg, and letters received home from superior officers stated that these men were among the best soldiers in the service, gallantly charging in direct assault as well as doing effective sharpshooting and picket duty. Although being dispossessed at home, they fought as valiantly under the Stars and Stripes as their ancestors did under the plumes of the wild American eagle, and let it be said in all justice that they cast a glamour over the annals of the North that shall not easily be effaced.

Of the hundred men who left to fight for their country, more than half were killed in battle and practically all the rest were wounded. At the present time there are but two survivors.

Lieut. Garrett A. Graveraet, who recruited the Indians and organized the company, brilliantly led his men in a daring charge at Spottsylvania after seeing his father shot dead at his side. At Petersburg, he was badly wounded in the left arm and died the first day of July following at Army Square Hospital, Washington, D.C. Lieut. Graveraet was a talented young man, an accomplished artist and a splendid musician. He was one of the first government teachers of the Indians at L'Arbre Croche and had great influence among the natives. Always honorable and straightforward in his dealings with them, his confidence was never betrayed and "My Indians," as he loved to call them, proved true and lasting friends. The remnants of the little band were among the first to enter Richmond to share in the great victory the North had won.

An amusing incident is related of Antoine Tabayant, one of the members of the Indian company. Twins, two boys, were born to him, after he had gone to the front, and Mrs. Tabayant at once wrote to her husband asking what names should be given them, for in the Indian custom it was the father's sacred prerogative to christen his sons.

Antoine answered immediately to call one Abraham Lincoln and the other Jefferson Davis.

His wife did as requested and the twins grew up to be lively youngsters; but sad to relate, both died before Antoine returned home from the war.

He did not know it, however, and as soon as he met his wife, after being mustered out, he inquired about the boys.

Sorrowfully the mother informed him of their death.

For a time the old warrior was disconsolate; but finally he summoned up courage and asked for particulars; how they had behaved, what they had done, and all about them.

"Well," replied Mrs. Tabayant, "they were always fighting. I couldn't turn my back but what they would be pulling one another's hair, clawing and biting and banging each other in the nose and eyes."

Antoine pricked up his ears. "Which one was the best man?" he asked blandly.

"Oh, Abraham Lincoln was always on top," answered his wife. "He could throw Jefferson Davis down, blacken his eyes and make his nose bleed every time."

The soldier's face lit up with a broad smile. "By golly, that's purty gosh darn good!" he exclaimed. "Jus' like I tole them fellers down South, aroun' Richmond—'You'll never find a Jefferson Davis that can lick one of our Abraham Linkum's."

"THE KING OF THE STAR" OR THE LEGEND OF MACKINAC ISLAND

According to an old tradition a party of Indian warriors were standing on the hill at the present site of St. Ignace, gazing out over the waters, when to their surprise they saw a huge object rise to the surface. It proved to be the island of Mackinac; but it so much resembled a large turtle that the Indians pronounced it, at the time, to be one. Its ancient name Michilimackinac signifies "giant turtle."

The island has always been clothed in mysticism and romance and is the very abode of legendary lore. Upon its rocky cliffs rollicking fairies danced, sang and laughed away their lives.

It is said that after the Great Spirit had created the island be placed it in the care of kindred spirits of the earth, air and water and told them it was to be forever the abiding place of peace and quiet. He was so pleased with the place in fact that he said he would make it his own home whenever he sojourned upon the earth.

The principal legend of Mackinac Island as related by the older Indians was as follows:

A poverty-stricken old man of the North by the name of Osseo took for his bride a slip of a girl who had nine sisters all married to handsome young men.

Her relatives laughed when they heard of the unusual match and predicted that this union of December to May would never prove happy.

But the girl was unmoved by their jeers and only replied: "I have made my choice and we will see who has acted wisest in the long run."

Shortly after the marriage the entire family started out one pleasant afternoon for a walk through the wood. All the bride's sisters and their husbands turned pitying glances at Osseo's mate.

"Too bad," said the oldest, "that our pretty little ne-she-ma (sister), had to marry that crippled old man. What a blessing it would be if he could stumble over a root and fall and break his neck so she could have a handsome husband like the rest of us."

In spite of this talk the young bride continued good-naturedly to help her husband along as best she could and bestowed upon him fond caresses and many acts of kindness.

Suddenly Osseo stopped at a large hollow hemlock log and looking up into the sky shouted: "Sho-wain-ne-me-shin, Nosa" (Pity me, my father).

Then darting into one end of the log he emerged from the other a handsome young brave, bearing the totem of the turtle. With light steps and joyful heart he took his wife by the hand and made his way to the head of the procession; but alas! she now was an old woman, bent and haggard, scarcely able to walk.

When Osseo saw what had taken place he was dumbfounded and nearly crushed with sorrow. With bowed head he led his wife back to his former position in the rear of the others; but he was very kind and considerate to her as she had been to him during the period of his own enchantment.

After a while the party came to a lodge and entered it to prepare some food. When all were inside, the others noticed Osseo withdraw to an open space a little ways from the lodge and again address himself to his father in the skies. Soon sounds were heard as of far-off music and a voice spoke to the young man as follows:

"Osseo, my son, I am conscious of your afflictions. I have heard your prayer and therefore summon you to come and dwell with me in the heavens where there are no trials nor tribulations. Leave your earthly habitation which is filled with sorrow, pain and disappointments. I have listened to your entreaty because you were ridiculed and abused by your companions. At the hollow hemlock I overcame the spell that bound you—the work of an evil spirit that resides on a neighboring star. Never let his beams strike you for they are the weapons he uses to work his wicked designs. He has enchanted your wife for a little while, but be not alarmed for I will dispel his power over her also. Arise, my son, and bring all your friends with you. Here your possessions will be turned into gold and silver; joy and contentment will be your constant attendants. I will clothe you with the beauty of the starlight and endow you with the knowledge and wisdom of a great Manitou. Come, for the King of the Star is calling you to everlasting happiness."

No sooner were the words uttered than the lodge began to career and rise into the air. Osseo's relatives ran to the door to jump out but were too late—already they were high above the trees. Then the lodge assumed the form of a cage and the inmates became various birds of beautiful plumage-robins, blue jays, red birds, canaries, humming birds, parrots, orioles and flamingoes, and Osseo's wife was transformed into a turtle dove, the most handsome and lovely bird of all, called O-me-me. But she did not long retain this form for the King of the Star returned her to her husband with all her former youthful grace and charm.

Osseo was then instructed to hang the cage with its captives at the door and to enter with O-me-me into the new realm to enjoy themselves forever. They lived on the star for many years and a son was born to increase their happiness. He proved to be a great favorite with his grandfather, the King of the Star, who indulged him in every way. One day the boy learned that shooting with a bow and arrow was the favorite pastime on the earth below and lie longed for one of the weapons. So the King of the Star presented him with an outfit and the birds were liberated from the cage that he might try his skill.

His very first shot brought down a beautiful white owl, but when he went to pick it up, behold! it was one of his aunts with an arrow sticking through her heart. The moment that pure and spotless star was stained by her blood the spell was dissolved. Slowly the cage and its occupants began to sink to the earth. The birds again assumed their natural forms but were so much reduced in size that they resembled fairies. At last they landed upon the Island of Mackinac where they have since resided, giving rise to the name "Fairy Island."

In Indian they are called Mish-in-e-mok-in-ok-ong, or "turtle spirits," and frequently they may be seen dancing on the pinnacles of the rocks and cliffs. Their voices may be heard at times, particularly on quiet moonlight nights, as they sing their refrains in homage to the King of the Star.

SUPERSTITIONS OF THE
STRAWBERRYAND BLACKBERRY

After the first man and woman were created they lived
in happiness for a time, but as all husbands and wives have
done ever since, they soon began to quarrel. At last it became so unpleasant in the wigwam that the woman decided to leave her husband and started off toward the land
of the setting sun.

After she had been gone a little while the man sat down
sorrowfully in front of his camp fire to think it over. Where-
upon the Great Spirit looked into his heart and seeing that
he was sad asked him if he would like to have his wife
back again.

He replied joyfully in the affirmative and promised
that if she were returned to him he would never quarrel
any more.

So the Great Spirit caused a patch of delicious huckle-
berries to spring up by the side of the woman as she walked
along; but she passed them by unheeding. Then he scattered in turn raspberries, sand cherries, gooseberries,
whortleberries and wild fruits of many kinds and descrip-
tions along the pathway; still the woman remained
untempted. Finally as a last resort the Great Spirit created
a patch of strawberries, the first of their kind. Upon seeing

them the woman immediately stopped to gather some and owing to her delay her husband had time to overtake her. Then she presented him with some of the choicest and they returned home together.

The Indians call the strawberry Odamin, which means "heart berry." It figures conspicuously in their mythology.

———————

The legend of another popular berry runs as follows:

The prickers on blackberry vines were caused by the burial of a very wicked warrior who had unjustly tormented a rival and his intended bride. His victim at last left the country with a war party and nothing was heard of him for weeks.

Then one day the wicked Indian appeared to the maiden and told her that her lover was dead—that he had been ambushed and scalped by the Sioux. The story was only a fabrication but the shock so preyed upon the girl's mind that it caused her death.

When her lover returned from the war and learned the truth, he challenged his rival to mortal combat. He was killed in the mêlée and buried by the side of his sweetheart. Then his friends revenged him by killing his enemy. The latter was buried between the other two graves—the reason assigned being that as he had come between them while they were alive, it was but meet that he should repose there after death as a continual reminder of his crime.

His spirit seeking release from its terrible anguish strove to arise from the grave but could only cling to the blackberry brambles about the mounds and its wickedness produced the prickers with which these vines have since been covered.

THE MOCCASIN FLOWER

When the first union between a white man and an Indian woman took place, the parents of the bride were greatly angered. They ordered the white man out of the village and told their daughter that if she did not leave the paleface they would disown her forever.

The husband, thus forced to leave, started away in his canoe in great sorrow, but his wife, true to her vows, followed along the shore all one day trying to call him back. As dusk came on she lost her way and fell in a faint and all night long the owls echoed her calls to her banished husband. The next day, flowers resembling her moccasins, were found all along her track. These are the white lady slippers. By her side was her babe held tightly in her death grasp. The Indians called them "Ko ko, ko ho moccasin," which means "owl shoes."

THE HANGING OF WAU-GOOSH

Away back in the early part of the last century there occurred in northern Michigan a public execution which attracted widespread attention. A scaffold was erected on Mackinac Island and a large crowd, numbering several hundred, assembled to witness the hanging of a bad Indian. The criminal was a bandit Ottawa who had killed many whites and terrorized the country about the straits for a generation.

The Indians for the most part had accepted the ways of their white brethren and were becoming more or less civilized; but not so with Waugoosh, "The Fox," who absolutely refused to recognize his new masters. In his youth, his family bad suffered wrongs at the hands of the hated invaders, and Waugoosh could neither forget nor forgive. His disposition was altogether different from that of his conquerors—his sole ambition centered in revenge.

How many white people he had dispatched with his tomahawk nobody knew, but it was said to be a large number. When some hunter was ambushed and murdered, or a helpless woman attacked and scalped while unprotected in the home or field, the authorities knew it was the work of Waugoosh. The few sheriffs and deputies then in the region were authorized to capture the desperado, dead or alive, and a big reward hung over his head. Nevertheless, by his native cunning and crafty plans he continued his bloody work and evaded the authorities for many years.

One of the crimes charged up against Waugoosh was the butchering of an entire English family that had sought to establish a home in the wilderness near Thunder Bay. The Indian killed the father and mother in a most brutal manner; then took the five young children, and, stringing them on a pole, hung them in the crotch of two trees. There he said they would dry and turn into toads, which he claimed would be a fit termination for all white people. Other acts equally as cruel filled the bloody pages of Waugoosh's history.

But at last the criminal was captured by a party of hunters after an exciting fight in the forests of Mackinaw county; and in order to set an example to all Indians inclined to question the supreme authority of the government, it was decided to hang Waugoosh in the public square.

The renegade, undaunted and seemingly unconcerned, followed the officers and hangman to the gallows. Just prior to the execution he was asked if he had anything to say. To this question he responded in his native tongue as follows, the speech being translated for those present by Madame La Framboise who was engaged for the purpose:

"I have killed hundreds of white people and know that I deserve to be punished. I don't expect any leniency; neither do I ask any. At the time I committed these murders I did not know it was wrong; I thought I was doing my duty and the more scalps I took the happier I seemed to be. But through the instruction of your priest I now realize that what I did was very wrong. I am therefore exceedingly sorry and wish to say to all my people that they should obey the laws and not seek to kill others as I have done.

"Long ago I was taught that every white man was my enemy; that I should ask him no favor and grant no quarter. Now all this has changed. I understand this new belief. I see that the Great Spirit intended us to live in peace on the earth, and not fight nor quarrel. For all this knowledge I am grateful to your priest. My last wish is for the Indians to be good citizens of this country which has passed permanently into the hands of a new race, no doubt for a wise and good purpose. I have repented of my sins and now I shall die happy, fully believing that the wonderful Redeemer of the white man is also the Great Spirit of the Indian and that He will not turn His back when we ask to be forgiven."

WHY CAMPFIRES CRACKLE

The Ojibway Indians thought that the thunder was caused by thunder birds that nested first in the region of Lake Superior and later, after the white man came, in the Rocky Mountains. When these birds winked their eyes they made the lightning, and the thunder was the roar of their wings as they sailed through the upper regions of the atmosphere. They often passed overhead on their way to and from the ocean where they went for serpents and fish.

These huge birds sailed so high that they could not be seen, but once one of them swooped down and caught a great hunter, who had lost his way in the forest, in its talons, and soared away. It took him to its nest on a high cliff where a number of the young birds began to peck the man's head. This so angered him that he commenced to battle with them and finally he overcame the flock. Then using the skin of one as a covering, he spread out the wings and sailed to the spot where he had first been captured, bringing with him the hearts of the young birds. These he put in the fire and burned up when he got back to his village. As they burned they made a crackling noise and jumped about on the coals. So, afterwards, whenever the fire crackled in the lodges of the Indians they said it was the noise that originated by the burning of the hearts of the young thunder birds.

Since then the birds belonging to this species are never seen, but are often heard far up in the skies. Their tears, as they mourn for their young, dampen the earth.

ENGLAND'S REVENGE

No trouble has been experienced by our government or any of the white people with the Indians of L'Arbre Croche since Pontiac's Conspiracy. That contest witnessed their last resort to arms, undertaken for the purpose of punishing the English for having defeated their great father, the king of France.

The result of the Conspiracy proper, however, did not break their power, though it declined shortly afterward. What really proved to be their undoing has always been charged by the Indians to an act of treachery and revenge on the part of the British. We have many times heard the rumor—it was a favorite topic among the older Indians. The reason the story does not appear in history is probably because the missionaries had abandoned L'Arbre Croche at that period and there was no one left to write the sad details.

No doubt we can best preserve the tradition by relating it in the words of an old brave who told it to the author personally:

"A long time ago," he said, "a tall pine tree with its top branches bent toward the east, stood on the shore a little ways north of Good Hart and was cherished by the

Indians as a famous landmark. It disappeared about one hundred years ago. Another grew in its place which was cut down by a bad man fifty years later. The offender had a miserable existence after that and died suddenly. He was punished by the Great Spirit because the Crooked Tree was sacred to the Indians. All the country surrounding it bore its name of 'Wau-go-naw-ki-si.'

"At the time of Pontiac the Ottawas in the region were as numerous as the leaves upon the trees and the great chieftain, who was himself an Ottawa, invited them to join him in his efforts to drive out the English. Many responded to his call because they loved the French people and regretted their defeat. After the war was over the English sent emissaries to L'Arbre Croche with presents and invited the headmen to Montreal for a council.

"There they gave them more presents in token of supposed friendship and as the chiefs were about to depart presented them with several silver boxes which were not to be opened until they reached their native village.

"The chiefs cheerfully consented to the request and brought the boxes safely home where they distributed their contents, consisting of trinkets, ornaments and gewgaws, among their people. Soon hundreds and hundreds were seized with fever and died in great agony for the boxes contained smallpox germs and were sent by the English for the purpose of punishing the Indians for having aided Pontiac. That is why so many bones and skeletons were found near the surface of the ground, especially at Old Middle Village where the first mission was established, about a mile south of the present Middle Village.

The Indians died so rapidly that they could not be properly buried and nearly all the survivors scattered in terror to other parts of the country. They came back in time, but never again did they regain their former prestige."

ORIGIN OF THE NAME "CHICAGO"

Evidently the name "Chicago" is of Algonquin origin. The Ottawas have the word, "She-gog" which means "a little furred animal with a strong odor," commonly known as a "skunk." But granting this to be the root of the name, where does the third syllable "o" come from?

After interviewing dozens of Indians regarding the matter we find the following story related by Chief Ogemaw of Good Hart to be the accepted version:

According to this authority, a white man—"No, not exactly a white man," explained Chief Ogemaw in his narrative, "but maybe it was an Irishman," was trapping near the Chicago river at an early day. He "jumped" a she-gog, which ran to the river and started to swim across, but sank in mid-stream never to reappear. The Irishman pursued it to the river bank where an old Indian was pitching his wigwam.

"What kind of an animal was that?" asked the Irishman.

"She-gog," grunted the old man.

"Where did it go?" inquired the trapper peering up and down the stream.

"The old man pointed to the river bottom and replied: 'That's where the she-gog go.'"

Although this story or variations of it is related by many Indians, nevertheless the writer questions its authenticity. He thinks it a pure invention, probably originating with some early trader.

More likely the name Chicago was derived from the term "chica-go-e-sheeg," an Ottawa word signifying "leeks" or "wild onions." The full name "Chicago" appears therein, the two last syllables being dropped for brevity's sake. It is said that there were many wild onions in the vicinity of the Chicago river in former times.

REV. J. B. WEIKAMP

Who established the Cross Village Convent

FATHER WEIKAMP'S SEPULCHRE

Built soon after he came to Cross Village in the middle of the last century

AN INDIAN CHIEF AND DAUGHTER

SUNSET ON LITTLE TRAVERSE BAY

Northern sunset scenes are magnificent and especially enjoyable at Bay View and Petoskey. The above was taken from the Petoskey breakwater.

INDIANS IN CAMP AT MACKINAC, 1870

THE OLD FORT AT MACKINAC ISLAND

OLD INDIAN TRAIL AT MACKINAC ISLAND

IN THE MURMURING FOREST NEAR HARBOR SPRINGS

Photo by Troup

FATHER PAUL—GOOD FATHER AND PRIEST TO THE INDIANS AT CROSS
VILLAGE FOR MANY YEARS—STAGES A PAGEANT OF OTTAWA BRAVES AND
SQUAWS IN FULL REGALIA AND WAR COSTUME

MIDDLE VILLAGE

The site of ancient L'Arbre Croche as it is today. Near here stood the famous Crooked Tree. There are records mentioning L'Arbre Croche Mission as early as 1695.

Photo by Troup

OTTAWA MAIDEN

ALONG THE SHORE AT PINE LAKE NEAR CHARLEVOIX

INDIAN MISSION CHURCH

Built about 1833 and still standing at Petoskey. Oldest public
building in northern Michigan south of the Straits of Mackinac

THE BEACH AT WEQUETONSING

Harbor Point, which, according to the legend, was at one time an island, is seen in the distance. From Wequetonsing, Petahsega set out on his flight of discovery to the happy hunting grounds.

CATHOLIC CHURCH AT CROSS VILLAGE

Marquette Cross in rear

AN INCIDENT OF EARLY MACKINAC

In the olden days the Indians reserved the riparian rights about Mackinac Island and during treaty payment times always pitched their tents and wigwams along the shore. It was a common sight to see hundreds of tepees strung along the beach, but the debris that resulted was an annoyance to the fashionable ladies of the island.

Upon one occasion some of them went to the Indian agent and made a complaint. They were so insistent about the matter that the agent called the Indians together and told them they would have to stop throwing their fish bones upon the beach.

"What do you want us to do?" asked the chief, "Eat the bones and all?"

"No," replied the agent, "you don't have to do that, but instead put them in bags and take them away with you."

The Indians were very sullen as they left the meeting and it is said some were so incensed over this seemingly absurd request that when they departed from the island in their canoes, they threw the bags of fish bones inland as far as they could.

LEGEND OF HARBOR POINT

The Indians of L'Arbre Croche were once ruled by a great chief who resided on the isle of Mackinac, and who went by the name of Potch-i-nong.

This great chief possessed supernatural powers and was greatly feared by his subjects who obeyed and honored him in all things. He ruled his people with a mighty hand and woe to him who dared disobey his commands.

Besides his earthly subjects, Potchinong presided over many fairy beings who came and went at his bidding and who made his home merry with their shouts and laughter. The loveliest of these strange beings was Wa-ka-sa-mo-qua, the chief's only daughter, who was as pleasant and kind as she was beautiful. But unlike the rest of her proud companions, she used to mingle with the people of the earth, much against her father's wishes. Potchinong had always boasted of his fine blood and bravery and said he would rather see his daughter killed than to have her marry among the mortals. He was a manitou (spirit) as well as a chief. Wa-ka-sa-mo-qua, however, continued her visits to the earth and fell in love with a young chief, Wen-de-ba-jig, handsome and brave, who resided on the mainland.

Potchinong learned of the disgraceful affair, and summoning his daughter, told her that she must stop all nonsense with the young chief and thus prevent dishonor and disgrace from falling on the family. He had already given his daughter's hand to a noted southern Motchi Manitou who was wealthy and powerful like himself; but the girl was as bent in her inclination as her father, and would not hear of her marriage to this evil one.

In vain did Potchinong interpose. Wa-ka-sa-mo-qua loved Wen-de-ba-jig and did not hesitate in telling her father that she intended to marry him.

Finally Potchinong, seeing that he could not dissuade his daughter, decided to have her paramour put to death.

Wa-ka-sa-mo-qua learned of her father's evil determination, and when night had folded its mantle over the Fairy Isle, she went with all haste to her lover and informed him of what she had heard, and enveloping him in a cloud she rendered him invisible and immortal. They then embarked in a canoe and made their way to the western shores of Me-ne-shance, "little island" (now Harbor Point), in Little Traverse bay.

Here they lived in happiness for many moons, but one evening when Wen-de-ba-jig had returned from the chase across the bay, his canoe loaded with the game he had slain, he was amazed to find a deep pool where his lodge had stood, and upon the bank, smiling derisively at him, was the Motchi-Manitou. He told Wen-de-ba-jig that he had taken his wife to dwell with him beneath the wave, but promised the pleading husband that he would return her when the island and mainland should become connected by solid ground.

Wen-de-ba-jig at once set to work upon the task that would restore to him his faithful wife, for a manitou no matter how bad, will never break his word. A many centuries of toil the tireless worker succeeded in making the island and mainland one, with the exception of the spot where the pool stood, which from its great depth was known as the "Devil's Pond," and the filling of which was a task beyond the power of Wen-de-ba-jib, who like Sisyphus of old rolling the stone forever, never ceased in his arduous labors.

The Motchi Manitou's voice could often be heard from the pond shouting mockingly at the indefatigable toiler and, until it was filled by the refuse from a saw mill that was located near by, it was necessary to quell his spirits by occasional incantations and the firing of volleys into the water, accompanied by other ceremonies of "shooting the devil."

The evil spirit long since disappeared, no doubt discouraged by the introduction of modern machinery and when the last load of sawdust was dumped into the Devil's Pond, the happy union of the separated couple can be imagined.

THE LEGEND OF THE WATER LILY

The Ojibways took precedence over all other tribes in the richness of their legendary lore and traditional tales. One of their best known legends is that regarding the water lily.

Once a young warrior noticed a star which seemed to be much brighter and nearer the earth than any of its companions. Upon going to bed the young man dreamed that the star descended and remained suspended in the air before him in the form of a beautiful maiden, who spoke as follows:

"I desire to live with the people of the earth. Show me a place where I can take up my habitation."

The young man suggested to her a place up in the trees.

"No," she said, "I would not be happy there. I would have only the birds for my companions. I would prefer to be nearer the ground where I can come in contact with the mortals of the earth whom I have learned to love."

The young man then suggested other places, along the hillside, in the valleys, or by the cliffs and rocks.

"None of those places will do, so I will select my own home."

Thus saying, she descended to the water nearby and dropped out of sight in its depth.

The young man in sorrow darted to the spot where she had disappeared, in the hopes of rescuing her.

There he saw only a beautiful white lily into which the maiden had been transformed.

These lovely flowers have ever since been found in and around the waters of the north.

OLD MAN WINTER

In a dark, deep and dangerous forest, once lived an old man, alone, and even woodland friends he had but few. The winter had been unusually cold and severe. The old man had suffered with the intense cold in spite of the warm skins he clothed himself with. One day, he found he could not leave his cabin, the snow being too deep and the air too cold.

And in his great despair, he called upon the Great God, Manitou, for aid. In answer to his prayer, the North Wind blew back the covering from the cabin door and, lo and behold! there entered a beautiful maiden, her head wreathed with the most fragrant of pink flowers, which warmed and perfumed the air about her. On her feet were moccasins of white lilies, and her robes were of ferns, sweet grasses, budding leaves and blossoms.

The old man looked upon his visitor with wonder, for he knew she had been sent in answer to his prayer, and, being powerful and gifted with magic himself, unless subdued by the enraged elements, he understood she was equally as powerful in magic; for hadn't the Great God, Manitou, sent her.

He bade her welcome and asked who she might be, and at the same time telling her that he too was great, for his breath could freeze up the streams; one nod of his white head would cause the leaves to fall from the trees and the forests and plains become carpeted with snow; he had but to walk about and the birds would leave in great flocks for the South, the animals seek their dens in great fear.

She, being unafraid, replied that her breath would cause the flowers to spring from the earth in joy and cover the woods and plains; a shake of her curls, the soft rain falls, the brooks are no longer frozen, the birds return and the animals stalk forth in great gladness, the leaves burst forth and the great woods is filled with songs of joy and gladness.

The old man was now growing too warm and sleepy. Manitou felt that he had been powerful long enough and that the fair maiden should reign for a long time to come. She looked down on the sleepy one and listened; the call of the bluebird came; the sun looked down on the melting snows; the stream began to murmur; the South wind sang its song to the awakening trees; all of the out-of-doors was glad and joyous.

The old man grew very small and slept on soundly.

The maiden laid vines of waxy green leaves and fragrant pink flowers, like those she wore in her hair, on the ground. Then softly she stole away, and from every print of her moccasined feet there sprang the lovely arbutus, each a tribute to her magic in causing sleep to fall upon the old man Winter.

HOW THE MOON AND STARS CAME

Formerly the rabbit was a beautiful and graceful animal, having no superior in personal comeliness in the forest. But one bright day it came out into the open to lie down and sleep in the warm sunshine.

At that time the sun was larger and brighter than it is today and it beat down upon the poor rabbit so fiercely that it burnt off his tail and bent his legs out of shape.

The little animal was awakened by the scorching sensation and jumped up and hopped around in great anger.

At that time the rabbit carried little magic pellets which it threw at its enemies to destroy them.

Resolving to avenge itself upon the sun, the rabbit traveled to the end of the earth and when it got as near as it could it threw one of its magic pellets at the great orb and struck it full in the face. This caused a great combustion and broke off a large piece which lodged in another part of the sky and became the moon, and the sparks flying in every direction from the explosion filled the firmament with stars.

Since that time the rabbit never comes out of its hiding place in the day time, but at night it sallies forth to play and gambol, because it is not afraid of its friends—the moon and stars—which it created.

EARLY HISTORY OF THE LITTLE
TRAVERSE BAY REGION[1]

Some idea of the habits and customs of these Indians when they were first visited by the whites, may be obtained from an article by Father Menard, one of the early missionaries who labored so zealously and who endured so many hardships to spread the Gospel among the Indians of this region. He says:

"There is a false and abominable religion similar in many ways to that of some ancient pagans. The Indians here do not acknowledge any sovereign Maker of Heaven and Earth. They believe that there are many Manitous, some of whom are beneficent, as the sun, the moon, the lake, the river and woods; others malevolent, as for instance, snakes, dragons, colds, storms; and in general, all that appears to them useful or injurious, they call a manitou, and they render to such objects the worship and veneration which we give to the true God alone. They invoke them when they go to hunt, to fish, to war or on a voyage.

"I have seen an idol set up in a village, to which among other presents they offered ten dogs in sacrifice that this false god might vouchsafe to banish elsewhere a malady which was depopulating the village. During storms and

---

[1]   Reprinted from "The Ottawan" by John C. Wright

tempests they sacrifice a dog to the Lake, which they throw into the water saying: 'Here is something to pacify thee; be still!' For the rest, as these people are dull, they do not acknowledge any deity purely spiritual. They believe that the sun is a man, and the moon is his wife; that snow and ice are also human beings, who go away in spring and come back again in winter; that the devil dwells in snakes, dragons and other monsters; that crows, hawks and some other birds are manitous and talk as well as we do, pretending there are some Indians who understand their language, just as some of them understand a little French. Moreover they believe that the souls of the departed govern the fishes of the lake and hence at all times they have believed in the immortality of the soul, even holding the doctrine of metempsychosis—that is the transmigration of the souls of deceased fishes, for they believe that they again pass into the bodies of other fishes. For this reason they never throw the remains from fish they have eaten into the fire for fear of displeasing the shades of those fishes, so that they might not come into their nets any more."

L'Arbre Croche Mission

(Harbor Springs)

Who the first explorer was that entered Little Traverse Bay is not definitely known. It was probably one of the early French *Voyageurs* who traded with the Indians of the

Mackinac country. Perhaps Nicholas Perrot who stayed at Mackinac Island about 1665 and who made frequent visits along the coast in different directions, was the discoverer of Le Petit Travers.

It was about the time of Pere Marquette's residence at Point St. Ignace, that the first mission was established on the shores of Little Traverse Bay, although by whom it is not known. Father Marquette went to St. Ignace in the spring of 1671 with the Huron Indians who were driven away from the mission of the Holy Ghost at La Point de St. Esprit, Chequamegon Bay, at the western end of Lake Superior, by the Nadouessi, a warlike tribe of Indians who inhabited the banks of the Mississippi river.

The mission at Little Traverse Bay may have been established by Father Dablon, who built a chapel at Michilimackinac the winter before Marquette's arrival there.

Whether there was a resident priest at the mission at the start we cannot ascertain, but if there was he probably did not remain any great length of time. In 1695 we find that it used to be attended by the fathers stationed at Mackinaw, and the baptismal records are still preserved at St. Ignace. The first entries are of 1741, and the last of 1765, by Father du Jaunay, acting Curé of Michilimackinac.

Probably the reason there was no resident priest at Little Traverse Bay is because there were not so many Indians at that point as at the other missions. However, the number steadily increased as the surroundings were favorable. Fish and game were abundant and many of the Indians had fields of corn. They were also very ingenious and made baskets, mats and bags from the bark of the basswood tree, which were handsomely colored with dyes they made from roots and barks they found in the vicinity. They also made many useful articles from birch bark. But though they were somewhat more advanced than other nomadic tribes they were very superstitious. Seven miles west of the mission on the banks of a small stream, was a large wooden idol painted and bedecked with feathers and other finery which they worshiped and to which they offered sacrifices. This was as late as Father Baraga's time in 1831 and '32. The chapel was located on the north side of the Bay, at the present site of the Catholic Church of Harbor Springs, and was known as L'Arbre Croche Mission. L'Arbre Croche village proper was located about thirteen miles further up the coast and at one time was the largest Indian village south of the straits of Mackinac. It was at that point where the Menominees, Chippewas and Ottawas held council, in July of 1763 after the massacre of Fort Michilimackinac, when the Ottawas had with them several English prisoners.

In 1825 Rev. Father Peter de Jean arrived in the Little Traverse region and built a church at Seven Mile Point; but as it proved unsatisfactory, the mission was moved to the site of the old L'Arbre Croche mission where a little log church—"prayer wigwam"—was built by Father de

Jean in 1827. During his stay at the new L'Arbre Croche Mission Father de Jean conducted a day school for Indian children.

On the 21st day of April, the mission was taken charge of by Father Baraga, who arrived from Cincinnati. A few weeks later Bishop Fenwick came and installed the zealous priest as pastor. "Happy day," says he, writing to the Leopoldin society, "happy day, which has placed me in the midst of the wild Indians, with whom I will stay, if it be the will of God, until my last breath be drawn."

He was well liked by the Indians and held services in the little church morning and night. He was assisted by an Indian Chief who read aloud from an Indian prayer book. Father Baraga lived in the greatest poverty. His pastoral residence was a rude log hut covered with bark, and when it rained he was compelled to spread his cloak over his books and papers to keep them from getting wet. It is said of him that he felt happier than a millionaire in his palace. During his stay at the L'Arbre Croche Mission he baptized 461 Indians. In 1832 he printed an Ottawa prayer and hymn book. He left the mission in 1833 and afterward labored at different points on the upper peninsula. In 1853 he was consecrated Bishop of Sault Ste. Marie, the L'Arbre Croche Mission being in his diocese.

A long list of priests succeeded him at L'Arbre Croche, Father Pierz and Father Zorn each remaining a long term of years.

The old church that attracted so many tourists in later years was erected about 1839.

One of the priests, Father Lantishar, who was at the mission from 1856 to 58, afterward went to northern Minnesota, and was frozen to death on the ice while attempting to cross the lake in midwinter.

During the summer of 1884 the Franciscan fathers were given charge of the mission.

The cemetery was formerly located back of the church, but a few years ago every foot of space was used and a tract of land was purchased north of the village. The old cemetery was an odd looking spot. The Indians profusely decorated the graves with artificial flowers made into wreaths and crosses, and also hung them in great profusion on the little white-washed fences surrounding the mounds.

The little village which grew up about the mission was given the name of Little Traverse, taken from the French name of the bay, Le Petit Travers, upon which it is situated. In 1851, continuous operations relating to the village began when Richard Cooper arrived and opened a small general store. From that time the white population has had a steady growth. A number of old implements and ancient articles have been unearthed near by, showing that this region must have been inhabited at some early date by a class of people quite highly advanced in civilization—probably the mound builders.

For a number of years the village was of exceptional importance because of its being headquarters for the payment of the treaties made with the Indians of this section, and hundreds of natives flocked to the place each year to receive their annuities from the Government.

In 1881 the town was incorporated and the name changed to Harbor Springs, which was suggested by its two leading advantages. The town now has a population of about two thousand.

Petoskey

The next mission to be founded on the shores of Little Traverse Bay was at Muh-quh Se-bing (Bear River) now Petoskey, on the south side.

The Indian village on this side of the bay was originally at Muh-quh Ne-bi-sing (Bear Lake), the source of Bear River. It was founded by three Ottawa Indians Pa-ba-ma-sha, The Sailor; A-ne-moose, Little Dog; and Moon-a-ba-tum.

The first Indian to locate at the mouth of Bear River was Sa-ga-na-qua-do, Rising Cloud, about 1825. Shortly afterward the village at Bear Lake was moved to the mouth of Bear River. The Indians never settled very thickly at this point on the Bay. Up to 1851 nothing of importance transpired, when a few Indian families moved there from old Mission on Grand Traverse Bay. Shortly after this Mr. P. Dougherty, who was conducting Presbyterian school at

Old Mission was requested by the Indians to start a school at Bear River. He at first declined but was afterward prevailed upon to visit the place, which he did in 1851-52, making a favorable report to the Board of Missions under whose authority he was acting. The Board accordingly appointed Mr. Andrew Porter, a former teacher at Old Mission, to take charge of the new school, which he did in 1852. With much difficulty he succeeded in erecting a small building on what is now the Jarman Farm, west of Petoskey. Mr. Porter found the Indians kind and friendly, he never having to turn a key to prevent their stealing. He reposed the utmost confidence in them. Their principal living was "min-da-min-a-bo," or corn soup. They took great interest in their school and many learned to read and write. After the Government established Indian schools this one was adopted, and Mr. Porter was paid a salary as teacher. In 1871 the funds set apart for this purpose were exhausted and the mission was abandoned.

In 1865, Hazen Ingalls, the first permanent white settler, arrived and purchased a little mill, which was built by a nephew of Mr. Porter in 1862. Mr. Ingalls immediately set the mill in operation and opened a little trading store, the first business place on the south shore of Little Traverse Bay. The year 1873 viewed the commencement of the metropolis of the Little Traverse region, which was named Petoskey in honor of Neyas Bedosega, an Indian who owned all the land in the vicinity. His last name translated means, "The Rising Sun," a fit name for the city that now casts its rays of influence over the entire region. The same year the Post Office was moved to the new settlement, Fox, Rose and Buttars commenced selling goods in a little log cabin, and shortly afterward the G. R. & I. Railroad was finished to this point. The general settlement of Emmet County was delayed on account of its lands being held subject to Indian treaty, but when, in 1874, the eastern townships came into market, and two years later the remainder of the county was opened for settlement, the village entered upon its great career. Since that time the growth of Petoskey has been phenomenal. It is now a city of about four thousand inhabitants and has justly been termed "The Pearl of the North."

Harbor Point

As soon as a way was opened to Little Traverse Bay from the cities, many tourists were attracted to its shores by the beauty of the surrounding country; resorts were established and attractive cottages erected. Each summer brought hundreds of people who sought the healthful climate and invigorating breezes of the bay.

One of the first resorts to be permanently established was on a point which curves gracefully into the bay directly in front of Harbor Springs, and thus forms one of the best harbors on the Great Lakes. The resort was named Harbor Point.

This beautiful bit of land was first purchased from Indians by Rev. John B. Weikamp, a Franciscan monk, who came from Chicago in 1855 for the purpose of establishing a mission for the Indians. He paid $100 for the piece of ground. He afterward found it was insufficient for his purpose and moved to Cross Village.

The first resident of Harbor Point was C. R. Wright, of St. James, Michigan, now a respected citizen of Harbor Springs[1]. He moved to Harbor Point in 1853 and engaged in the cooperage business. His house and shop were located near the end of the Point. He remained there until 1856 when he went back to St. James.

In 1878 the land was purchased by a company incorporated as the Harbor Point Association, and opened as a resort the following year. Harbor Point is now covered with handsome cottages and is the pride of Little Traverse Bay.

We-que-ton-sing

We-que-ton-sing is a picturesque spot one mile east of Harbor Springs. The resort comprises about eighty acres of land donated to the Presbyterians by the citizens of the latter place. In 1877 a Presbyterian committee which met at Elkhart, Indiana, accepted the gift and the resort was established under the name of The Presbyterian Resort.

---

[1]   Mr. Wright died at Harbor Springs in July, 1901.

The Indian name of the place was Wa-ba-bi-kang, meaning a white, gravelly shore. The place was afterward called We-que-ton-sing, which was taken from the Indian name for Little Traverse Bay.

Cross Village

Cross Village is situated on Lake Michigan about sixteen miles north-west of Harbor Springs, and is a small town of about 325 inhabitants, mostly Indians. The popular belief is that the first mission was established there by Pere Marquette, but this is not known for a certainty. Probably the formation of the belief lies in the fact that the Indians say that it was established by "Kitchimekatewikwanaie," the Great Priest.

When the explorers first landed at Cross Village a large cedar cross was erected on the hill, from which the town derived its French name, La Croix, in Indian, A-na-mi-a-wa-tig-on-ing. The Indians say it was placed by their request over the grave of a chief whom they greatly loved. The old cross has long ago succumbed to the elements and another erected in its place, about two rods from where the first cross stood. This one also has been replaced several times, so that it would be impossible to find the exact position of the first cross. The present one is probably the fifth or sixth.

Who the first priest was that had charge of the La Croix mission is not known. Indian tradition says that the first priest at La Croix was well liked and converted many of their number. It was probably Reverend Father du Jaunay. He stayed at La Croix nearly one year, and thinking that he had sufficiently civilized the Indians, he decided with their aid to celebrate Corpus Christi in an appropriate manner. A large number of the L'Arbre Croche Mission Indians were invited to attend the ceremony. They arrived at La Croix the evening previous. During the night two Indians became involved in a quarrel over a girl. The members of the two missions took sides and a terrible massacre ensued. When morning came the priest gazed in horror on the dead bodies, and washing his hands of the affair, he embarked in a canoe and left the spot forever.

When the Catholics returned and re-established the abandoned missions in the Little Traverse Region in 1825, a church was built at La Croix by Father de Jean. The history that is left of the mission is very meager. The village at that time was located below the hill.

The old church which now stands near the center of the village[1], was erected about 1848 by Father Mrak. The last priest to have charge of the Mission was Father Sifferath in 1868.

In 1875 the name of the town was changed from La Croix to Cross Village.

---

[1]   Destroyed by a fire that swept Cross Village in October, 1918.

GLOSSARY

A few Words and Phrases with Their Ottawa Equivalent

Ache—We-sug-e-naz-e-win.
Apple—Me-sheem-in.
Ashes—Bung-we.
Aunt—Ne-noo-sha.
Automobile—Gay-jeeb-e-zood dob-on.
Boy—Skin-ne-gish, or Quee-we-sance.
Basket—A ko-ko-be-naw-gun.
Boat—Chemon.
Butter—Zowa bimeda.
Candy—Ze-ze-baw-qua-donce.
Cat—Gaws-a-gance.
Coat—Beeska wagun.
Cow—Bi-sha-ka.
Cruel—Maw-jay yaw-wish.
Crying—Maw-wi-win.
Cucumbers—Ash-kit-a-mo.
Day—Keej-ick.
Dog—Mo-kaw-gee.
Doll—Dum-min wau-gun.
Eagle—Ma-gizzy-wass.
East—Wa-ba-nong.
Eat—We-sin.
Flower-Wau-wass kona.
Flowing well—Mo-ki-tun.
Girl—Qua-sance.
Goat—Gitchi wa-bo-zoo.
Hand—O-ninge.
Hen—Bah-kaw-qua
Homely—Mah-nah-de-za.

Horse—Baji-go-ga-ji.
Ill-Awkozy.
Indian—Nish-naw-ba.
Knowledge—Ki-kane-dah-mo-win.
Laughter—Bop-a-win.
Look—Naw bin.
Lover—Ne-ne-mo-sha.
Man—A ninny.
Meat—We-oss.
Money—Show-nee-ah.
Noon—Now-o-quag.
North—Ke-way-di-noong.
Own—koko koko
Pigeon—O-me-me.
Plum—Bugy-sawn.
Pretty—Qui-nage.
Quick—Way-weeb.
Rabbit—Wau-bo-zoo.
Resorter—Ne-bin nish-e-jig.
Road—Me-kun.
Robin—Pit-che.
South—Shaw-wah-noong.
Spring—Me-no-ka-mig.
Squirrel—A-jid-a-mo.
Summer—Ne-bin.
Tomorrow—Wau-bung.
Town—O-da-now.
Trousers—Me-kin-node.
True—Dabe-wa-win.
United States—O-da-na-win

Utensil—A no-cause o-win-nun.

Winter—Be-bone.

Well or spring—Mona bawn.

Wood—Me-sun.

White man—Che-mok-e-mon (Big Knife).

West— A-pung-ish-a-moog.

Going down hill—Ne-saw-ki.

Going up hill—O-gie-daw-ki.

Go away—Wush-ti-ba.

Come with me—Maw-chon.

Hello or good-by—Bo-jo.

Let us play golf—O dum nin no dah, ma tig gonce, bah quock ko donce.

Do you love me?—Ki zah gay, e nah?

Let us have some fun—O sawn a ways e dah.

Do you dance?—Gi neem nuck ko?

Are you hungry?—Buck a day, nah?

Lots of fun—Onona goozy win.

A moving picture show—Ba baw mo say, mi zin itch it gun, ma mon jeen o win.

I should worry—Dah niece shane dum.

How old is Ann?-Ah nee dush, Ann, Ah peet ah zid.

War is hell—De bish ko an naw ma kom mig, me god a win.

It's a nice day—Me no ki she gut.

Come again next year—Me na wah beshawn ne-bin.

Be careful—Wing gay zin.

Good luck—Me no say.

Rainy weather—Gim me one.

Certainly—Ah neen da.

Michigan signifies "a clearing" and was first applied to the northwestern shores of lower Michigan where there were large ancient clearings. The Indian pronunciation is Mashiganing.

Mackinac comes from the Indian word Mishinimakinang and means "big turtle."

Wequetonsing—"Little bay." By the Indians Harbor Springs was and is still called Wequetonsing. What is now Wequetonsing resort was called Wa-ba-bi-kong, which means "a white gravelly beach."

Petoskey—"Rising sun" or "coming light."

Traverse City—Gitchi Wequeton—"Big bay."

Detroit—Wa-wi-ah-ti-nong.

Chicago—"Place of wild onions," not skunk, as some claim.

Grand Rapids—Bah-go-ting.

Mississippi—"Large river," pronounced in principal Algonquin dialects. Me-she-se-be.

Cheboygan comes from the word sha-bo-e-gun-ing and means "going through."

Sing gog—Harbor Point—"A beautiful point."

St. Ignace—Nad-a-way-qua-yam-she-ing.

Charlevoix—Ma-daw-be Bah-de-noong—"A passageway down to the bay."

Way-ya-ga-mug—"Round lake."

Wau-go-naw-ki-sa—"The crooked tree." This was the name given to the country from Harbor Springs (Wequetonsing) to Cross Village.

Ah-na-may-wa-te-going—Cross Village.

Ah-pi-tah-wa-ing—Middle Village.

Muckwah ne bod—"Sleeping Bear."

Muckwah zeba—Bear River (now Petoskey).

Muckwah ne bissing—Bear lake (Walloon).

We-que-naw-bing—Bay View.

Sheem-a-balm-a-kong—Seven Mile Point.

Chippewa—Bah-go-ting—Soo river rapids.

Ah-mik-ko-gane-dah—Beaver Island.

Ching-walk-go-ze-bing—"Pine River."

Pit-tik-way-wi-ji—"Roaring Brook."

Zebewaing—Five Mile Creek.

Tim misk o nush qua ze wom—"Idylwilde."

May Gwa ah qua had da bay—"Forest Beach."

Waugoshance—"Little fox."

Skillagalee is not an Indian word but comes from the French "Isle aux Galet—"Pebble Island."

Good Hart—Post office and store near Biddle Village. The store is the old government school building, one-fourth mile from The Crooked Tree.

Bliss Farm—Me-sheem-in Naga-wash-ta-kwa-ko-sid—"Short Apple Tree."

Burt Lake—Sha-bo-e-gun-ing.

Crooked Lake—We-gwas-sance-ka-ig—"Lots of little white birches."

Lake Superior—Gitchi Gum-ing—"Big lake."

Lake Erie—Named for the tribe of Eries or Cat nation on its south shore.

Lake Huron—From the Huron or Wyandotte tribe.

Ne-saw-je-won—"Water running down"—A term applied to the chain of rivers and lakes from Superior to the Atlantic.

Green Bay—Bo-gee-we-quade.

Milwaukee—Min-newog—"A nice place."

Wisconsin—Wish-konsing—"Place of rushes or reeds."

Les Cheneaux Islands—Cheneau in French means "young oak"—the Indians call them Nom-i-nong.

Northport—Michiganing—"A clearing."

Ludington—Na-na-da-be-ga-gan-ing—"Boney like."

Grand Haven—Wash-tenong.

Muskegon—"Fresh smelling."

St. Louis, Mo.—Me-she-ze-bing—"City on the big river."

St. Joseph, Mich.—Potta-wotto-me-nong.

Frankfort—Ka-she-za-ing—"Flying fast."

Canada—Shaw-ga-nosh-king—"British land."

Buffalo—Be-she-ka Wah-ka-kaning—"Wild Cow Country."

Niagara Falls—Ne-beesh A-bung-ge-sing—"Failing water."

Manistee—Sba-wa-noong, (south) A-nom-i-nit-i-noong.

Manistique—Ke-way-di-poong, (north) A-nom-i-nit-i-noong.

Mackinaw City—Gata Oda-noong.

Bois Blanc Island—Wego-bemish—"White wood" island.

Round Island—Me-ne-sa-sing.

Manitoulin Island—Manitou waning—"Spirit land."

Quebec—Ka-bek.

Montreal—Money-ong.